Moving On Facilitator's Guide is accompanied by a number of printable online materials, designed to ensure this resource best supports your needs.

Go to https://resourcecentre.routledge.com/speechmark and click on the cover of this book.

Answer the question prompt using your copy of the book to gain access to the online content.

T0383526

"The *Moving On* series gives all who work with children a powerful, practical tool to help them 'leave well so they can enter well'. As each book focuses on a particular stage of the moving process, children can find words and create images to express the often-paradoxical feelings any move can make. I highly recommend it!"

Ruth E. Van Reken, co-author of *Third Culture Kids: Growing Up Among Worlds*

Moving On Facilitator's Guide

Moving On Facilitator's Guide is designed to accompany the *Leaving Well* and *Arriving Well* activity books. Based on the latest relocation and transition research, the guide builds the confidence of adults in delivery of the activity books to share wellbeing boosting strategies for transition and beyond, both for the child and the supporting adult.

This practical guide offers guidance notes and prompts to help bring out the best experience for the child. It will help the adult feel confident in responding to any questions, including key points to consider and examples of 'what you could say'. It goes on to explain the theory behind the activities from the workbooks and includes examples and quotes from other ex-pat children woven through the text.

The guide can be used effectively with:

Leaving Well Activity Book which helps children to reflect on how they feel about the move, to remember other moves and understand that change is a part of life.

Arriving Well Activity Book which can be used on its own or following on from *Leaving Well* and continues to move through this process, helping the child to settle when they have arrived in their new country.

Inspired by research, this invaluable guide will help teachers, practitioners, and parents support children on the move to leave and arrive well.

Claire Holmes is Head of School Counselling at Tanglin Trust School, Singapore where she leads a team of counsellors who work across the whole school K-13. Claire's counselling modality is strength-based, empowering others to access their own inner wisdom and knowing. Her practice incorporates expressive therapies, mindfulness, and solution-focused interventions. In her role, she teaches mindfulness-based stress reduction (MBSR) to parents and staff.

Moving On Facilitator's Guide is part of a set – *Moving On: Activity Books and Guide to Support Children Relocating to a New Country.*

Book 1 – *Leaving Well Activity Book: Therapeutic Activities to Support Kids Aged 6–12 who are Moving to a New Country.*

Book 2 – *Arriving Well Activity Book: Therapeutic Activities to Support Kids Aged 6–12 who have Moved to a New Country.*

Book 3 – *Moving On Facilitator's Guide: How to Support Children Relocating to a New Country.*

Moving On Facilitator's Guide

How to Support Children Relocating to a New Country

Claire Holmes

Routledge
Taylor & Francis Group

LONDON AND NEW YORK

Designed cover image: Claire Holmes

First published 2024
by Routledge
4 Park Square, Milton Park, Abingdon, Oxon OX14 4RN

and by Routledge
605 Third Avenue, New York, NY 10158

Routledge is an imprint of the Taylor & Francis Group, an informa business

British Library Cataloguing-in-Publication Data
A catalogue record for this book is available from the British Library

ISBN: 978-1-032-46684-2 (pbk)
ISBN: 978-1-003-38284-3 (ebk)

DOI: 10.4324/9781003382843

Typeset in Helvetica Neue LT Std
by KnowledgeWorks Global Ltd.

Printed in the UK by Severn, Gloucester on responsibly sourced paper

Access the Support Material: https://resourcecentre.routledge.com/speechmark

Dedication

Dedicated to my companions on my global adventuring: My husband, Chris, my two Third Culture Kids, Hana and Ben, Neo the Scottie Dog and Milo the tabby cat.

Acknowledgments

Heartfelt thanks to my Tanglin Trust School Counselling Colleagues, past and present; Kendra Frazier, Valerie Hoglan, Paula Huggins, Pippa Gresham, Simon Parkin, Seunghee Chung, Jo Bush, Kevin Dunk, and Tash McCarroll; you have been unflagging sources of wisdom, inspiration, and compassion. Lastly, deep appreciation goes to my wonderfully wise School Counselling Supervisor, Helen Wilson, thank you for being my guru.

Contents

Welcome   *xii*
How to use this book   *xiii*
Notes from the author   *xiv*

Leaving Well Activity Book

Page Title:	Page No. in Activity Book	Corresponding page No. in Facilitator's Guide
Welcome!	1	1
Where are you now?	2	4
Change happens.	3	6
Moving on graph.	4	8
Moving on takes GUTS[2]	5	10
People power.	6	12
Leaving things behind.	7	14
Lighten the load.	8	16
Feelings Faces.	9	19
Draw feelings out.	10	22
Talk feelings out.	11	25
And there's more.	12	27
Hopes and fears flower.	13	29
Who and how?	14	32
Staying connected.	15	34
What brings me joy?	16	36
What does my body tell me?	17	38
How do I cope well?	18	40
What encouraging things can I say to myself?	19	43
What's in and out of my control?	20	45
Mindful colouring.	21	48
Take 5.	22	50
Thankfulness Tree.	23	52
Stand like a tree.	24	55
Get curious.	25	58
Curiouser and curiouser…	26	60
Ballooning around.	27	62

Gallery of Strengths.	28	64
Moving on poem.	29	66
Moving on podium.	30	68
Coping Cube.	31	70
Awards ceremony.	33	72
My well-wishes.	35	74

Arriving Well Activity Book

Page Title	Page No. in Activity Book	Corresponding page No. in Facilitator's Guide
Welcome.	1	76
Your life-story.	2 & 3	78
Change happens.	3	79
Where are you now?	4	81
Feelings wheel.	5	83
Listen to your body and speak kindly to yourself.	6	85
Keep your breath in mind.	7	87
Ground yourself.	8	89
Moving on graph.	9	91
Pros (things that are going well) and Cons (things that are not going so well).	10	93
Mindful colouring.	11	95
Move your body to lift your mood.	12	97
It's wonderful and new.	13	100
Missing where you came from.	14	102
Top tip # 1: Be brave.	15	104
Top tip # 2: Be approachable and smile.	16	107
Top tip # 3: Keep curious (Your new environment).	17	109
Top tip # 3: Keep curious (New country report).	18	111
Top tip # 3: Keep curious (Similarities and differences).	19	113
Top tip # 4: Be yourself.	20	115
Top tip # 5: Be kind (Kind to others).	21	117
Top tip # 5: Be kind (Kind to Self).	22	119

Top tip # 6: Be grateful.	23	122
Top tip # 7: Focus on your strengths. (What are strengths?)	24	125
Top tip # 7: Focus on your strengths. (Strengths that you take everywhere you go).	25	127
Top tip # 8: Remember your old place.	26	129
Top tip # 9: Make your bedroom a haven.	27	131
Top tip # 10: Ask for help.	28	133
Moving on podium.	29	136
Instructions for making a 'Wellbeing Boost Game'.	30	138
Wellbeing Boost Game.	31	140
Awards ceremony.	33	142
Brain-dump page.	35	144

Bibliography   *145*
Index   *146*

Welcome

Moving On: Activity Books and Guide to Support Children Relocating to a New Country

A very warm welcome to you. It's wonderful you have chosen the Moving on Series to support transition to a new country. There are three books in this series:

Book 1: *Leaving Well Activity Book: Therapeutic Activities to Support Kids Aged 6-12 who are Moving to a New Country*.

Book 2: *Arriving Well Activity Book: Therapeutic Activities to Support Kids Aged 6-12 who have Moved to a New Country*.

Book 3: *Moving On Facilitator's Guide: How to Support Children Relocating to a New Country*.

The Activity Books: The content of these books has been crafted to fit with research on the process of transition, relocation, and cultural adaptation. You may be wondering why Book 1 is *Leaving Well* and Book 2 is *Arriving Well*. This is because how well you leave a place directly impacts how well you enter. Both activity books are designed for 6–12-year-olds. The simplicity of design is deliberate to encourage the child to colour, decorate, and annotate the book to be their own, allowing them to be an active participant in their move. It is recommended that children are introduced to Book 1 at around eight weeks before departure and Book 2 on arrival in the new country.

Book 1: This activity book helps kids reflect on how they feel about the move, to remember other transitions and understand that change is a part of life. Engagement with the text normalises mixed feelings, helps the child acknowledge their hopes and fears and reflect on their sense of control. A relocation graph is included to help the child understand the typical responses to stages of transition. The text acknowledges change is stressful, the child is encouraged to think about their own responses to stress and build their coping repertoire. The concept of GUTS[2] is introduced, an acronym for five key things to address to leave well. The reader will explore what each of the letters stands for and consider how paying attention to these can help make their process smoother. The book concludes with activities that bring together the child's journey through the pages, helping to solidify their learning and engagement with the text.

Book 2: This activity book helps kids understand that transitions are a part of life and to reflect on how they feel. The book shares strategies to cope with change. A relocation graph is included to help the child understand the typical responses to stages of transition. The text prepares the child for the inevitable honeymoon period and dip in mood that most people moving to a new country experience. The text then guides the reader through ten top tips that will help arrive and settle well. These are valuable strategies to boost wellbeing as they move forward too. The book concludes with activities that bring together the child's journey through the pages, helping to solidify their learning and engagement with the text.

Book 3: This guide contains guidance notes, prompts, and bonus material for helping the facilitator bring out the best experience for the child using the two activity books from the *Moving On* series. The *Facilitator's Guide* can be used to support one child or a group of children by parents, teachers, learning support teachers, and/or counsellors. The support material helps the adult feel confident in their delivery and in responding to questions related to the discussion. Each activity page in Books 1 & 2 has a corresponding page in the *Facilitator's Guide* for the lead adult to refer to when delivering the material, each of which features:

- A page rationale which touches on the theory behind the activity.
- A visual of the corresponding page.
- Materials needed.
- How to set the scene.
- How to complete the activity.
- Facilitator's top tips.
- How to close the activity.
- Possible extension activities.

How to use this book

The material within the *Facilitator's Guide* is differentiated for supporting one child or a group of children. Some guidance is explicitly directed at parents, and some directed towards teachers/therapists. The lead adult is encouraged to choose the pace of facilitation, to deliver the pages in a different order, not to guide some of the pages, or to leave some pages out altogether. They may decide to present the material differently than suggested or change/remove parts of the activities or guidance. This way, the programme can be tailored to the needs of the target individual child/group. The facilitator may ask the child/ren to complete some pages in their own time, with or without an adult helping. Throughout the guide suggested scripts for the facilitator are highlighted in italics; these can be tweaked or changed to fit with how the lead adult would usually articulate. In essence this is a guide; the lead adult is invited to use it with discernment and flexibility. Each facilitator will bring their own flair and style to delivery. It is intentional that there is no approximation of time needed to complete each page; facilitators are best placed to decide timings based on the child/ren they are working with and how deeply they want to dive into the material. Some pages will have a lighter touch than others. The lead adult may encourage children to decorate their page as fully as they wish, adding their own style. This increases investment, for this reason, coloured pencils/pens are added to the material needed list, even though they may not be explicitly needed for completing the page.

Notes from the author

I am delighted you have chosen the *Moving On* Series to support moving to a new country. I've been working as a teacher and school counsellor in an international school setting for over two decades. In that time, it has been my pleasure to support children and families in global transition. The ebb and flow of leaving and arriving has fascinated me in my time abroad. I've tried my best to encapsulate my learnings in the two activity books that this guide accompanies. Here are some points to consider before getting stuck into facilitating these two texts. Please take what's helpful.

The key to a successful move for children is helping them prepare in advance. Being intentional about transitioning well ensures important parts of the moving process are not forgotten. How we leave a place greatly impacts how we arrive at the next. If we leave well, chances are we'll arrive well too. Moving is a time when children feel a lack of control; however, they feel empowered if they engage with their leaving process as much as possible. Change is unsettling, yet it is a part of life; resilience is built when children learn change is manageable.

Parents and guardians often ask, 'When should I tell my child/ren we are moving?' A general rule of thumb is, when parents/guardians know about the move for sure, it's time to tell the child/ren. In that conversation, it's important to let children know why the family is making the move. It's vital that children find out from their parent/guardians first to maintain trust. All children react differently when they receive the news they are moving, depending on their age and their affinity to their current country; this can vary from immense excitement to a complete reluctance to leave their home and social network behind and anything in between.

The child on the move will probably bombard the adults in their lives with questions and worries, or they might not; patience is needed. Encourage children to be involved in decisions with regard to the move as much as possible. Parents and guardians should give as much choice as appropriate about things both concerning the move and in general throughout this time of transition. Choice is empowering. Teachers and therapists should weave in as much choice as possible in their interactions with the child on the move too.

The GUTS[2] model, an acronym, provides the nuts and bolts of leaving well. A checklist of sorts is to enable a smooth exit (see image on the right). It's important the leaving child/ren understand the value of considering these five things as part of their leaving well plan. These are helpful things for parents and guardians to consider for their own transition too.

Moving on takes GUTS[2].
Goodbye – say your goodbyes
Unload feelings – share how you feel
Thank you – say thank you to important people
Self-Care – look after you
Say hello – think about your new country

For parents and guardians, do model acceptance about moving and be as positive as possible. Try not to talk negatively about moving, even if you are not sure about it yourself. Do encourage the child/ren to ask anything about the move, providing them with as much detail as you can. Help them see the positives and opportunities the move brings and listen to their perceived challenges too.

This is an important time for parents and guardians to boost self-care. The benefit of this is two-fold. Firstly, it models the importance of looking after oneself in busy and stressful times and may prompt the child/ren to follow suit. Secondly, when parents engage in self-care, particularly activities that rejuvenate, they can offer more measured and steady parenting.

If the child on the move asks to talk with you, stop what you are doing and engage; if it's not possible, tell them when you'll be able to chat. During conversations 'be there', keep eye contact, ignore distractions, come down to the child's level, and keep your body language open and relaxed. As you talk, look for cues about feelings and help the child to name those, listen to their words, tone of voice, and body language. Our natural response is to steer away from difficult emotions but calmly staying with what arises helps to get to the heart of the matter, making the child feel heard. Let the child do most of the talking, allow them to tell their story fully, and offer silence to allow them to go deeper. Resist the urge to 'fix' the problem; show you understand, value, and respect what they are telling you, even if their feelings are different to yours. Encourage the child/ren to understand that difficult feelings are temporary and that feelings change over time. Help child/ren to understand that it is normal to have uncomfortable feelings about a big change. Try to avoid telling children that it will be okay, not to worry or use statements like 'you don't need to be concerned about that' or 'don't be silly, it's going to be fine'. This minimises their experience and may prevent them from telling you their struggles moving forward. Sometimes it's hard to keep the conversation going, reflecting-back the details you heard and feelings they name can maintain flow. In your conversations, listen for the child's strengths and let them know you heard and appreciate them.

Normalising, validating, and empathising are useful conversational tools. Normalise, by letting the child know it's normal to feel this way. You might say, 'Moving is scary, it's normal to have tough days and feel sad sometimes'. Validate, by letting the child know they are heard and understood. You might say something like 'Gosh, that sounds tough, I can hear it's hard to think straight at the moment'. Empathise, by letting them know you see their perspective. You might say, 'I know how tough it feels when things are so busy, there's so much to do with the move and everything else, it's hard to manage'.

With older children, check in about the helpfulness of your conversations about the move; ask them, 'I hope that this conversation was helpful?' 'Can I do anything different to support you?' 'Let me know when you'd like to chat again, I'd really like to help'. This shows you are figuratively walking alongside them.

It's okay to let the child on the move, know you don't know how things will turn out, but you know they can cope, and you are there to support them. You might like to ask older children, 'Given how you feel, what's your plan?' This plants the seed that they are capable, resourceful, and you trust they will figure it out. Don't be afraid to relay your own experiences of change, focusing on what you learnt and the strengths you developed. Look out for times the child copes well and let them know that you noticed. Highlighting times of bravery and courage builds more.

Settling into a new country may take a while. Allow children to take the time they need to adjust to their new surroundings and lifestyle. On the left are ten top tips for arriving well. These are important things for 'the arriver' to consider. Parents and guardians, make time to connect with the community; take children to local activities, such as sports or cultural events; encourage connections with others and ways to get familiar with the new environment. If a new language is spoken in the new country, children may like to begin to learn some basic words; this may be something you do together.

Top Tips for Arriving Well
#1 Be brave
#2 Be approachable and smile
#3 Keep curious
#4 Be yourself
#5 Be kind
#6 Be grateful
#7 Focus on your strengths
#8 Remember your old place
#9 Make your bedroom a haven.
#10 Ask for help

One over-arching thing to note is that throughout this process of transition, relationships are paramount. The bedrock of being able to support fully is a kind, understanding, and ideally playful relationship. Parents and guardians, even though it's a busy time, prioritise time spent with your child/ren, actively engage in activities and times of just being. This will help the child feel safe through the transition. Teachers, check in with the child more often than usual. Parents, guardians, and teachers, if you feel that the child's daily functioning is being impacted by the move, do seek extra support.

It's hoped the two activity books, whilst designed for the child on the move, hold many helpful transition pointers for faciltators too. If you are embarking on a global transitition yourself, good luck and bon voyage; if you are supporting a child to either leave or arrive, they are very lucky to have you. However, you have come to be facilitating these activity books, may you find them helpful, engaging, and thought provoking. My wish is that you have as much fun delivering them as I did creating them. Go well; dream, explore, and discover.

Leaving Well Activity Book

Page title: Welcome.

Page no: 1

Page rationale: This page welcomes the reader, stating the book's purpose and what to expect from the *Leaving Well Activity Book*. The text plants the seed that if you leave well, chances are you'll arrive well too. The child begins to take ownership of their process by writing their name and sharing a little about themselves on their page.

Page visual:

> ## Welcome!
>
> You've been given this book because you are moving to a new country. Each page has a different activity. You'll get creative by drawing; colouring, writing, and making things.
>
> It's a book that helps you learn about leaving well. If you leave well, most likely, you'll arrive well too. Using this book will help you have a good last few weeks and make a great start in your new place.
>
> My name is _____
>
> I am moving from _____ to
>
> _____
>
> ①

Materials needed: Each child needs: Pen, pencil, rubber, sharpener, coloured pens/pencils, activity book. Optional: World map/country floor labels.

Setting the scene: You may say, *'Welcome. You've been given this book because you are moving to another country. This book will help you leave well, and that means, most likely, you'll arrive well too. We are going to have some fun completing the pages; I'm here to help and answer any questions. If you are ready to get creative, let's begin… '.*

Completing the activity:

1) Read the two paragraphs on the page out loud or ask the child/ren to read it themselves.
2) Ask the child/ren to fill out their name and where they are moving from and to on the lines provided.
3) If you are a parent supporting your child, you may like to proceed to page 2 now. You may say, *'Let's turn over to the next page and get our crayons/coloured pencils/felt tip pens at the ready'.*
4) As teachers/therapists, if you are supporting one child, you may ask them where they are moving to and how long they have lived in their current country. In a group setting, there are various options; you may invite the children to share the country they are moving to out loud or in pairs. If the child/ren are shared in pairs, you might include an activity where they introduce their partner, telling the group their partner's name and the country they are moving to. Alternatively, you may get the students to imagine there is a world map on the classroom floor. Indicate where Australia and New Zealand are with the USA and Canada on the other side (you might use a visual of a world map, labels on the floor, or pure guesswork). Ask them to roughly position themselves where they are going. Ask the children to tell the group the country they are moving to from the position they are standing in.

Facilitator's top tip: Find a way to celebrate the diversity of countries you hear (if appropriate). You may say, *'Isn't it interesting hearing that you are off to such different places? That's what makes moving so interesting, everyone's story is different and special'.*

Closure: You may say, *'Thank you for sharing, I am really looking forward to hearing more as we move through this book. Let's turn over to the next page now and get our crayons/coloured pencils/felt tip pens at the ready'.*

Extension activity: You may like to ask the child/ren to count on their fingers how many countries they have lived in, including their current one. Ask them to hold their hand up to show how many fingers they have selected. Find a way for the child/ren to list the countries they have lived in. You may like to show your own number of countries you have lived in by showing the appropriate number of fingers too.

In a group setting, ask the students to raise their hand if they have lived in one country or more (all hands should be raised). Ask the students to keep their hand up if they have lived in two countries or more and to lower their hand if they have lived in one country only, then, keep their hand up if they have lived in three countries or more and to lower their hand if they have lived in two countries. Keep moving up number of countries in this way until only one student's hand is raised (or there is a tie). Invite group member/s with the greatest number to share the countries they have lived in.

You could also try this activity with students standing and sitting down when appropriate instead of hand raising and lowering.

*****

Leaving Well Activity Book

Page title: Where are you now?

Page no: 2

Page rationale: This page offers an opportunity to reflect. The child is invited to draw what best represents their current country inside a circle. A circle is a reoccurring theme in healing across many cultures. The experience of creating a circular, visual representation helps the child to acknowledge what had meaning to them in their current country. No two circles will be the same.

Page visual:

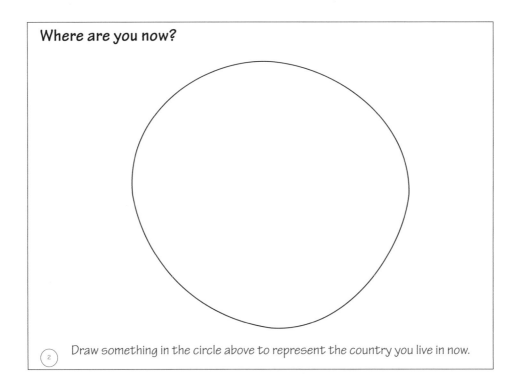

Materials needed: Each child needs: coloured pens/pencils and their activity book. Optional: White board or digital way to record responses, pictures of host country, printer, blank circles as needed.

Setting the scene: You may say, *'This page invites you to get creative by thinking about what best represents this country in a picture'.*

Completing the activity:

1) Before they begin ask, *'When you think of the country you live in now, what do you think of? What seems to best represent _____ (Add the name of the country here)?'* You can do this verbally or use a white board or digital medium to record responses.

2) You may like to give an example of what you would draw in the circle if you were the artist.

3) You may say, *'It doesn't need to be a perfect artwork. You can draw specific things or be more abstract using colours, shapes lines, or squiggles'.*

Facilitator's top tip: Have a variety of art materials ready. The child/ren may like to print out pictures to add; you may consider having some prepared for them.

Facilitator's top tip: Some children may take longer than others to do this task. If you feel that you'd like to move on before the child/ren have finished, do so, giving an option to finish their piece another time.

Facilitator's top tip: After you have set the scene and brainstormed ideas, this may be a page you ask the child/ren to complete in their own time. If you'd rather keep the book with you, give them a blank circle to take with them which can be stuck in later.

Closure: You may say, *'Thank you for using your artistic skills. I hope you are pleased with your creation'.*

Extension activity: You might like to ask the artist/s to give their piece a title. If you are working with one child, you might like to set up a role play; invite the child to pretend their artwork is in an exhibition. Tell them you are a visitor to the exhibition and challenge them, as the artist, to tell you the title and as much as they can about their piece.

In a group setting you may invite group members to introduce (using the art exhibition example above, if you wish) their artwork one by one, sharing the title and something brief about their creation.

Perhaps creating an interactive gallery of sorts appeals; you may like to get the children moving around the room, sharing their piece with another child, then moving to another when they are ready, or on your signal.

Another suggestion is to create a gallery by laying out the artworks for the group to view.

*****

Leaving Well Activity Book

Page title: Change happens.

Page no: 3

Page rationale: This page seeks to normalise change and help 'leavers' appreciate that transition is a normal part of life. The child is invited to recall and reflect on a previous transition. Remembering times of change and what was helpful increases confidence about the current move and the child's sense of self-efficacy to leave well.

Page visual:

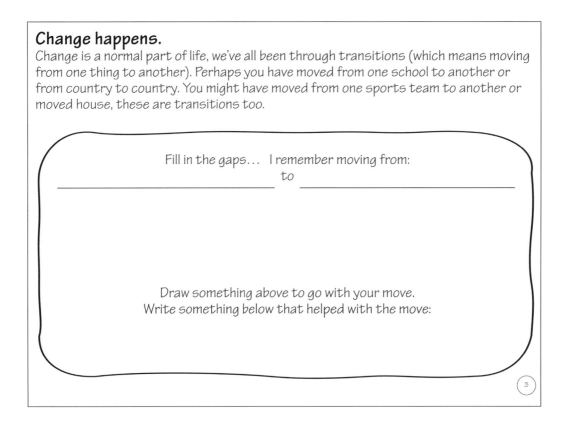

Materials needed: Each child needs: Pen, pencil, rubber, sharpener, coloured pens/pencils, activity book.

Setting the scene: You may say, '*This page helps to realise that change is a normal part of life. The good news is that human beings have the inbuilt ability to cope with change. Remembering a time when you moved from one thing to another may remind you of what helped last time*'.

Completing the activity:

1) You might like to read the paragraph at the top of the page aloud or invite the child/ren to read it silently to themselves.
2) You may say, *'Choose a time you moved from one thing to another and write what it was on the lines on the page. Draw something to represent the transition in the box and write something below your drawing that helped you'*.

Facilitator's top tip: Some children might need help with choosing a transition. If so, revisit the ideas in the paragraph or, if you are in a group setting, hear from others what they have chosen.

3) When the child/ren have completed their page, ask them to share as little or as much as they would like. You might like to do this in pairs if you are in a group setting.

Closure: You may say, *'Now we know that change is a part of life, let's look at how you might be feeling during this time of change on the next page'* OR if you are concluding for the session, *'Next time we return to this book, we'll look at how you have been feeling during this process of change'*.

*****

Leaving Well Activity Book

Page title: Moving on graph.

Page no: 4

Page rationale: The moving on graph describes a typical experience of relocating to a new country. The graph is based on the U-Curve Adjustment Theory coined by Norwegian sociologist Sverre Lysgaard in 1955. Since then, it's been used and adapted widely to help understand cultural adaptation. This page offers the opportunity for the child to locate themselves on the graph before and after they heard they were moving and allows them to reflect on their current emotional experience. This page looks to foster acceptance for whatever feelings are arising and normalise mixed emotions. Wellbeing is defined, a theme that runs through the book.

Page visual:

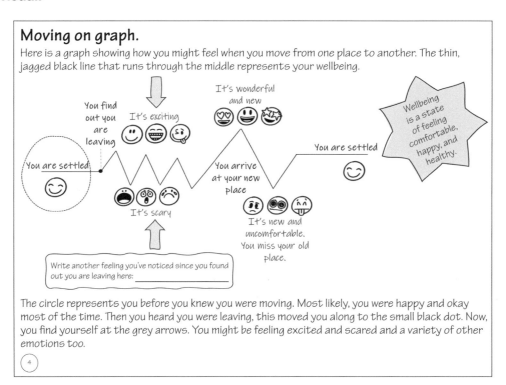

Materials needed: Each child needs: Pen, pencil, rubber, sharpener, coloured pens/pencils, activity book.

Setting the scene: You may say, '*On this page is a graph showing how you might feel when you move from one place to another. Everyone's experience is different but there are similar things that people notice when moving to a new country. Let's have a look at the graph*'.

Completing the activity:

1) You may say, '*The first thing to notice is the thin, jagged line that runs through the middle of the graph. That represents your wellbeing. Wellbeing can be described as feeling comfortable, happy, and healthy*'.

2) Get the child/ren to trace the line from left to right with their finger. Ask them, what they noticed about the line as they did this. (Draw out that the line moves up and down.) Let them know that wellbeing is like this, it's 'up and down'; some days you feel better than others.

3) Ask them to place their finger on the circle, ask them what it says inside the circle. When they reply, 'You are settled,' let them know this circle represents them before they knew they were moving. (If they ask what settled means, you may say, '*It's feeling comfortable with where you are*'.)

4) You may say, '*Then you find out you are leaving*', ask them to move their finger along to the small black circle.

5) Ask them to keep tracing with their finger until they get to the grey arrows. Ask, '*What happens to the line?*' (They will notice it goes up and down quickly/sharply). You may say, '*This is where you may experience a roller coaster of emotions. Perhaps, feeling sad one minute, excited the next and lots of other feelings too*'.

6) Ask the child/ren if they have noticed feeling excited or scared since they found out they are leaving. Explore responses. If you are working with one child, normalise their experience; if you are in a group setting and many indicate feeling these emotions, highlight the common experience.

7) Invite the child/ren to name another feeling they have noticed since they found out they are leaving. Ask them to write it on the line inside the box under the graph.

8) If you are supporting one child, invite them to share the feeling they have written with you. If you are supporting a group of children, you might like to invite them to share their feeling, if they wish, perhaps popcorn style (children share their feeling in random order by speaking it out loud).

Facilitator's top tip: You may like to have an additional resource availiable; a feelings wheel or list to help the child/ren name emotions.

Closure: You may say, '*Sharing feelings can feel uncomfortable, but doing so can help you feel more in control. Whatever you are feeling is okay, some feelings will be the same as others and some will be different. It's important to recognise that everyone's moving* experince is unique'.

Facilitator's top tip: If the child/ren ask you what unique means, you may say, '*Unique means special to you*'.

*****

Leaving Well Activity Book

Page title: Moving on takes GUTS[2].

Page no: 5

Page rationale: This page introduces the GUTS[2] model, an acronym, which provides the nuts and bolts of leaving well. A checklist of sorts enables a smooth exit. This page acknowledges that moving needs bravery.

Page visual:

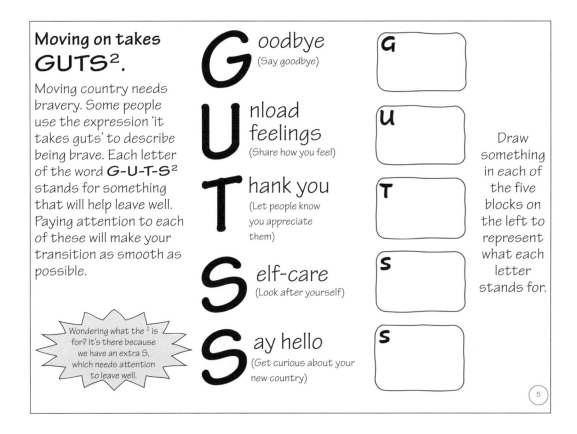

Materials needed: Each child needs: Pen, pencil, rubber, sharpener, coloured pens/pencils, activity book.

Setting the scene: You may say, *'You might have heard the expression "it takes guts" to do something brave'.* Ask the child/ren if they can think of a time that they were brave and invite sharing, as appropriate. In a group setting, you might use the popcorn method to verbally gather examples; the child/ren speak out their examples of bravery in random order.

You may say, '*Moving on needs bravery. Each letter of the word GUTS² stands for something that will help you leave well. Maybe you are wondering what the ² is for? It's because we have an extra S, so, let's start building our GUTS²*'.

Completing the activity:

1) You may say, '*The G is for Goodbye – this is about saying goodbye*'.
2) You may say, '*The U stands for Unload feelings – this is about sharing how you feel*'.
3) You may say, '*The T is for thank you – this is about letting people know you appreciate them*'.
4) You may say, '*The first S stands for Self-care – this means looking after yourself*'.
5) You may say, '*The second S stands for Say hello – this is about getting curious about your new country*'.
6) Ask the child/ren to close their books and recall what each of the five letters of GUTS² stands for.
7) Ask the child/ren to open their books to page 5 again and fill in the five blocks on the right with a doodle that represents each of the letters; their drawings can look like something specific or be abstract using colours, shapes, lines, and/or squiggles.
8) If you are supporting one child, you might like to ask the child to talk you through what they are drawing for each of the blocks and invite them to explain why. If you are in a group setting, you may invite the children to share with the person next to them as they are drawing.

Closure: You may say, '*In order to leave well you'll need to pay attention to each of these five blocks. This will make your transition as smooth as possible; the next few pages look at each of the five letters of GUTS² to help you plan how to do this*'.

Extension activity: Movement break: If you are in a group setting divide the children into five groups. Give each group one letter: One group gets G, another group gets U, and so on. Ask group members to join to make their letter shape using their bodies.

*****

Leaving Well Activity Book

Page title: People power.

Page no: 6

Page rationale: This page starts the journey through the GUTS[2] acronym with the first letter, which stands for Goodbye. An important part of leaving well is saying farewell to those people who have made a difference; this facilitates healthy closure. Interestingly, Douglas W. Ota says that goodbyes are often avoided as they are inherently painful in nature; however, he stresses their importance in facilitating optimal departure. This makes planning and preparation key. Pages 8 and 9 take inspiration from the work of David Pollock, Ruth Van Reken, and Michael Pollock, who highlight the vital four Ps of saying Farewell (people, pets, possessions, and places).

Page visual:

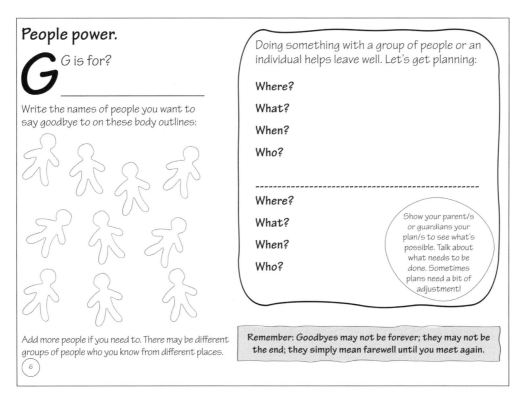

Materials needed: Each child needs: Pen, pencil, rubber, sharpener, coloured pens/pencils, activity book. Optional: timer, spare paper as needed.

Setting the scene: You may say, *'This page is called 'People power' because connections with others is such an important part of being human. Saying goodbye to those people who have made a difference in your time here helps leave well. There may be people from your* *neighbourhood, family friends, friends from activities outside of school along with school friends and school staff whom you'd like to say goodbye to. It may feel easier to avoid saying goodbye because it's difficult but identifying who those special people are, making plans and following them through makes it easier'.*

Completing the activity:

1) Begin by inviting the child/ren to fill in the blank, **G is for** _____ (Elicit from child/ren: Goodbye). Remind them that this is the first letter of GUTS[2].

2) Ask the child/ren to think of important people to say goodbye to. Ask them to identify 10 people, you might ask them to use their fingers to count 10.

3) Invite sharing of who their 10 people are with you or in a group setting, in pairs. You may use a timer to do this set for one minute to keep sharing focused and brief.

4) Ask the child/ren to write the names of their chosen people on the 10 body outlines on the left of the page.

5) Invite the child/ren to add more body outlines by hand if they need to. They may like to join people by lines or circles who they know from different places.

Facilitator's top tip: The child/ren may choose to write more than one name on the body outlines to represent a group of people.

6) Bring the child/ren's attention to the right-hand side of the page to the Where?, What?, When?, Who? You may say, *'We are going to think about how to say goodbye now. This is unique to you, everyone chooses a different way of doing this. It can be arranging something that costs nothing like a football match in a park, an event where you visit somewhere, a goodbye party or taking cupcakes to a last session or class. You've probly got lots of ideas of your own'.*

7) Invite the child/ren to fill in the Where?, What?, When?, Who? spaces choosing inviduals or groups, letting them know they can create more of these if they need to (you might have some paper ready for this as necessary).

8) Bring the grey box, bottom right of the page to the child/rens attention. Read the quote to the child/ren or ask them to read themselves. Encourage them to reflect on what the quote means to them. Draw out that there are lots of ways to stay in touch if they choose to.

Closure: You may say, *'Plans for goodbyes will need to be discussed with your parent/s or guardian as you will, most likely, need their help. Your plans may need to be adjusted, so, prepare to be flexible and open to ideas when you speak to them. Sometimes the planning part can be almost as much fun as the actual event'.*

*****

Leaving Well Activity Book

Page title: Leaving things behind.

Page no: 7

Page rationale: Douglas W. Ota highlights the nature of mobility and transition as a grief and loss process. We grieve things we have lost. Acknowledging what is to be left and having a plan of how to say goodbye gives a sense of agency at a time when things feel out of control. It also brings closure, facilitating the smoothest transition possible.

Page visual:

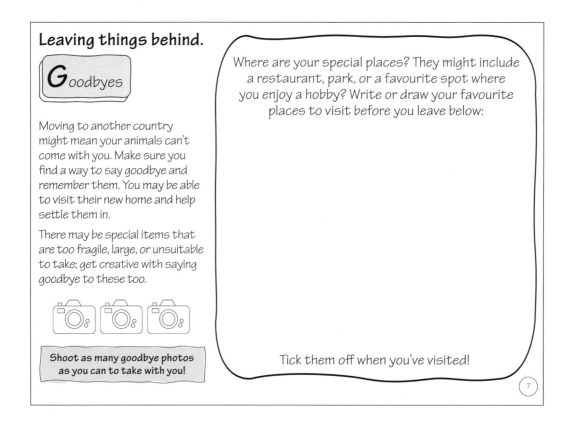

Materials needed: Each child needs: Pen, pencil, rubber, sharpener, coloured pens/pencils, activity book.

Setting the scene: You may say, *'When you move to your next country, there may be things you must leave behind and that can be hard. We are going to think about some of those things now so you can say goodbye properly'.*

Completing the activity:

1) You may say, *'The first thing that we will talk about is pets. There may be a beloved pet that can't make the journey to the new place'*. If you are supporting one child, ask them if that's true for them. If they have a pet going with them, ask them about that process; if they have a pet that they must leave behind, ask them about their pet (name, type of pet, how long they have had it, what they like about their pet). Be curious about where their pet will go and how they can be involved in that process. Encourage them to take photos, you may ask, *'Is there any other way that you could remember your pet?'* In a group setting, you may encourage them to have a similar discussion in pairs or ask the students to share verbally. You might do this using popcorn style to gather examples; the child/ren speak out their answers in random order if they choose to.

2) You may say, *'Next we will think about things that are too big, fragile, or unsuitable to take, what sort of things might these be?'* Gather answers of examples of such items. You may like to record the responses in some way.

3) You may share, *'One example of a heavy item that couldn't go with one family was a big sofa. The boy in the family was sad to leave the sofa; it had been with him for as long as he could remember. He decided to have a final mug of hot chocolate on the sofa to say goodbye. He even wrote a short poem about the sofa which he read as he sat on it for the last time. He took a photo of his "last sit" – printed it out together with the poem and took it with him on his next adventure'*. Help the individual/group to brainstorm some creative ways to say goodbye to the examples that you gathered in 2).

4) You may say, *'Next, let's think about saying goodbye to places'*. Bring attention to the right-hand box on the page, ask them to read the paragraph or you may read it aloud. Get them to write or draw the places they would like to visit one last time. Encourage them to tick places off as they go and to take lots and lots of photographs.

Closure: You may say, *'There's a lot to think about isn't there? Goodbyes can be exhausting but are an important part of leaving well'*.

*****

Leaving Well Activity Book:

Page title: Lighten the load.

Page no: 8

Page rationale: Transition research, most notably from the work of David Pollock, Ruth Van Reken, and Michael Pollock, highlight that reconciliation is an important piece of leaving well. This speaks to the notion that doing one's best to attend to any broken relationships reduces the chances of disputes becoming 'unfinished business', baggage, that is metaphorically carried into the next place. Harbouring resentment or regret may negatively impact new connections.

Page visual:

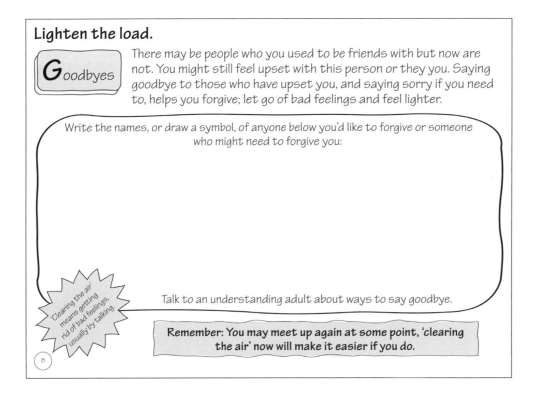

Materials needed: Each child needs: Pen, pencil, rubber, sharpener, coloured pens/pencils, activity book.

Setting the scene: Read the top paragraph of this page to the child/ren. You may add, *'Have you ever packed such a heavy suitcase that it's hard to carry? It's much easier when we travel light'*.

Completing the activity:

1) You may say, '*Most likely you can think of someone here who you've had a tricky time with. Let's fill in the box on this page. Write the name, or draw a symbol, if you'd prefer, of anyone you'd like to forgive or someone who might need to forgive you*'. If they can't think of someone, read the top tip below, if they can move onto 2).

Facilitator's top tip: Some children may say they don't have anyone to add to the box; let them know this is okay; they might think of someone at a later date and they can talk to you about it if they do. For now, encourage them to draw colours, shapes, lines, and/or squiggles in the box on this page to represent forgivness and making things right.

2) You may say, '*Let's think of ways to say goodbye to these people, even though it might be hard*'. You may elicit ideas of ways to say goodbye from the child/ren and record these in some way. The child/ren will most likely have some suggestions but if not, talk about things like speaking face to face, sending a card, sending an electronic message.

3) Ask the child/ren to think about what they would like to say to these people. You may say, '*You might like to let them know you are leaving, and you'd like to say sorry or let that person know that even though things have been tough between you wish them well*'.

4) Ask the child/ren to make a note of their preferred way of saying goodbye to each person they have added to their page.

5) You may say, '*Of course there is a chance that the person might not respond in the way you wanted or even respond at all. All you can do is your part 'clearing the air'. This is an important part of your leaving and arriving journey.*

Facilitator's top tip: The child/ren may ask you what 'clearing the air' means, or you may wish to check they understand this term. You may say, '*Clearing the air means getting rid of bad feelings between people, usually by talking to them*'.

Closure: You may say, '*For most people, this is one of the most challenging pages of the book to fill in and follow through with. If you need any extra help with it, do let me or another adult know. Even though it's a bit tough, it's such a useful part of your leaving and arriving well journey. Have you heard the expression, "the world is getting smaller"? That means that you might see people again, either in real life or online. The box at the bottom reminds us of that; it says, Remember, you may meet up again at some point, "clearing the air" will make it easier if you do*'.

'Thanks for using your courage to fill in this page today'.

Extension activity: You might find it useful to lead a movement break after this activity. An example would be getting the child/ren to stand up and lead them in a body pat down – gently using both hands to pat different parts of their body with their hands, starting with the head, moving down to the feet, and all the way up again. Encourage them to do this with kindness and gentleness to themselves.

*****

Leaving Well Activity Book

Page title: Feelings faces.

Page no: 9

Page rationale: This page begins the second letter of the GUTS[2] acronym: Unload feelings. Being able to name and share feelings has a regulatory effect. Research suggests that naming feelings reduces the force of emotion. Dan Siegel, Professor of Psychiatry at UCLA School of Medicine, coined the concept 'name it to tame it'. Naming the feeling helps reduce the intensity of emotion to feel less overwhelmed and more in control. This activity encourages the child/ren to explore a range of feelings and share them with a trusted adult. By understanding that all feelings are okay, the child/ren grow acceptance.

Page visual:

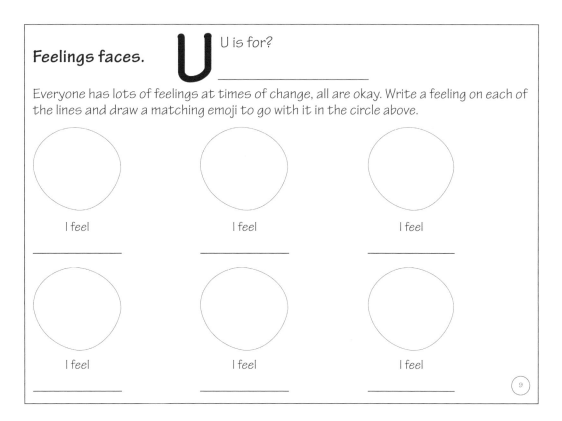

Materials needed: Each child needs: Pen, pencil, rubber, sharpener, coloured pens/pencils, activity book. Optional: Feelings list, white board, or paper to record responses.

Setting the scene: You may say, *'Now, we move onto the second letter of GUTS[2]. Can you remember what U stands for?* (Elicit from the child/ren: Unload feelings). *Sharing feelings can help leave well. Perhaps you've heard the saying, "A problem shared is a problem halved". This phrase is very true! Unloading feelings will help you cope better'.*

Completing the activity:

1) Begin by inviting the child/ren to fill in the blank, **U is for** _____ (Unload feelings). Remind them that this is the second letter of GUTS[2].
2) Read the top right paragraph out loud yourself or ask the child/ren to do so or you may ask them to read it silently.
3) You may say, *'I'm guessing you have lots of different feelings about moving, some might feel okay, and some feel uncomfortable'.*
4) Ask the child/ren if they can think of one feeling they have noticed at this time of change. If they can think of a feeling, move onto 5). If they are unable to think of one, follow the top tip below.

Facilitator's top tip: If the child/ren are struggling to identify a feeling, take them back to page 4 and talk about the examples of excited, scary, and the one they added. Or you may have a feelings list/wheel you can share with them.

5) Next, ask the child/ren to draw an emoji or feeling face in the first circle to represent the feeling they have identified.
6) When the child/ren have drawn an emoji, if you are supporting one child, you might like to be playful and try to guess the feeling that goes with the emoji before the child writes it down. In a group setting, you may try a similar game in pairs.
7) Ask the children to continue creating their emojis and naming them, they may complete a few or all. Continue with the guessing game if you wish.

Facilitator's top tip: Take opportunities to normalise feelings shared by saying something like, *'It's normal to feel that when you are moving, it's a big thing to cope with'.*

Facilitator's top tip: Take care not to label feelings as good or bad, rather as signposts that provide important information. Highlight that noticing and naming feelings helps to understand ourselves better.

8) When their page is complete you may ask, *'What do you notice about your page?'*, *'Were you surprised about any of the feelings?'*, *'Is there anything else you would like to share about your page?'* In a group setting, write the feelings on a board or

large piece of paper to demonstrate the wide variety. You may like to read them out loud and say, *'there are so many different ways to feel at this time of change and all are okay'*.

Closure: Some children may enjoy sharing feelings; some might find it challenging. If you have time, ask the children how they feel after drawing their feelings faces. To close, you may say, *'Noticing, naming, and sharing feelings is an important part of leaving well, thank you for telling me about your different feelings. It was interesting to notice the range of different emotions and see them drawn as emojis'*.

*****

Leaving Well Activity Book

Page title: Draw feelings out.

Page no: 10

Page rationale: Acknowledging and accepting feelings helps to cope better when tricky emotions arrive. This page invites the child/ren to engage with the qualities of a chosen feeling. It encourages a playful and curious approach for navigating the emotional landscape.

Page visual:

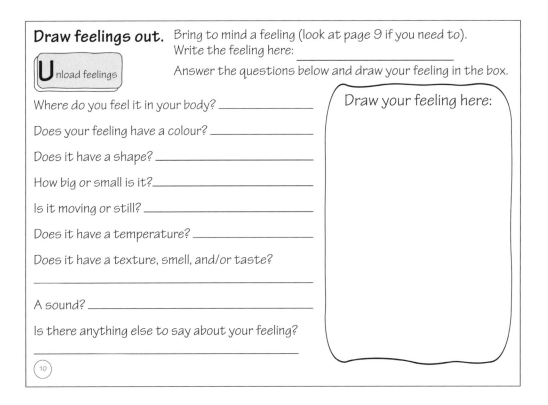

Materials needed: Each child needs: Pen, pencil, rubber, sharpener, coloured pens/pencils, activity book.

Setting the scene: You may say, *'Noticing, naming feelings and being curious about them helps us take good care of emotions and feel more in control. This page invites you to get curious about a particular feeling.'*

Facilitator's top tip: The child/ren may ask you what emotion means. You may say, *'Emotion is another word for feeling, both describe your emotional state'.*

Completing the activity:

1) You may say, *'Let's begin. Choose a feeling you'd like to explore. Turn to page 9 if you need help thinking of a feeling. When you have chosen a feeling write it on the line at the top of this page'.*

Facilitator's top tip: You may have an additional resourse available like a feelings wheel or list.

2) There are a variety of options for ways to answer the questions on this page. You may guide the child/ren through each question and invite them to write their answers on their page. In a group setting, the child/ren may complete this in pairs, interviewing each other, writing their partners answers for them in their book. Alternatively, you may offer a visualisation exercise with the child/ren recording their answers afterwards. If you choose the latter, you might like to follow the script for 'Exploring a Feeling Visualisation', below (if you choose NOT to do this exercise go straight to 4).

Exploring a feeling visualisation:

Facilitator's top tip: Some children will silently notice answers during this activity. Some may answer you aloud. There is no right or wrong way to do this.

Facilitator's top tip: The script below is designed to lead the child/ren whilst they are seated on a chair. Feel free to adjust the script if the child/ren are in a different position.

'Get yourself comfortable in your seat, adjust your body position a little if you need to.
Begin by closing your eyes if that feels comfortable for you.
As you sit here, notice your feet in contact with the floor. Be aware of your body sitting here in the chair, notice which bits of your body are in contact with the chair, notice which parts of your body are not.
Be aware of the air around you, notice if it's warm or cold, moving or still.
Notice your breathing, no need to change your breathing, notice the inbreath and the outbreath. Breathing in and breathing out. Notice how your body rises on the inbreath and falls on the outbreath.
Now, bring to mind the feeling that you'd like to get curious about. Name the feeling silently to yourself. Whilst you keep your eyes closed, I'm going to ask you some questions. Notice the answers that come, there is no right or wrong.
Where do you feel your feeling when it arises, in your body? (Pause).
If your feeling had a colour, what would it be? It may be one colour, more than one colour. Notice the shade of the colour is it bright, dark, or light? (Pause).
Perhaps your feeling has a shape? It could be a recognisable shape or something new. (Pause).

Notice how big your feeling is; is it big, medium, or small? (Pause).

Is your feeling moving or still? If it's moving, notice how it is; it might be fast or slow. (Pause).

Imagine that you could reach out and touch your feeling. Would it be hot, cold, or warm? As you reach out and touch your feeling, notice if it has a texture, it could be bumpy or smooth, soft or hard or furry. (Pause).

As you sit with this feeling, take a deep breath in and out. Does your feeling have a smell? It might even have a taste, notice what this might be, it could be a new taste or a favourite taste. (Pause).

Is there a sound that goes along with your feeling? (Pause).

Take another deep breath in and out. Do you notice anything else about your feeling? (Pause).

Letting your feeling go now. Knowing you can come back and connect with it anytime you need to.

Becoming aware of your breathing again, your inbreath and outbreath. Breathing in and breathing out, your body rising and falling. (Pause).

Becoming aware, again, of your body sitting here in the chair, the parts in contact with the chair and those not.

Notice your feet in contact with the floor.

Now gently open your eyes, come back into this room.

Facilitator's top tip: If time allows, you might like to ask the child/ren what they discovered during the exercise and invite them to share verbally.

3) Ask the child/ren to fill in the left-hand side of their page with the answers to the questions they discovered in the exercise.

4) Invite the child/ren to draw their feeling in the box on the right-hand side of the page. Let them know that it can look like something or be more abstract using, colours, shapes, lines, and/or squiggles.

5) Invite the child/ren to share their page and say as little or as much as they would like about it; they can do this with you or each other in a group setting.

Closure: You may say, *'Thanks for using your curiosity today. It's been interesting hearing about your feelings. Remember, getting to know feelings can help us feel more in control, which is especially helpful at times of change.'*

Extension activity: If time allows, invite the child/ren to share one thing that they'd like to remember after completing this page.

*****

Leaving Well Activity Book

Page title: Talk feelings out.

Page no: 11

Page rationale: Feelings that are not attended to may become stuck energy. Releasing feelings verbally by sharing with others is cathartic. This page helps the child/ren identify supportive people to talk to. This increases the chances of them choosing an emotional outlet through conversations with key 'helpers' at times of need.

Page visual:

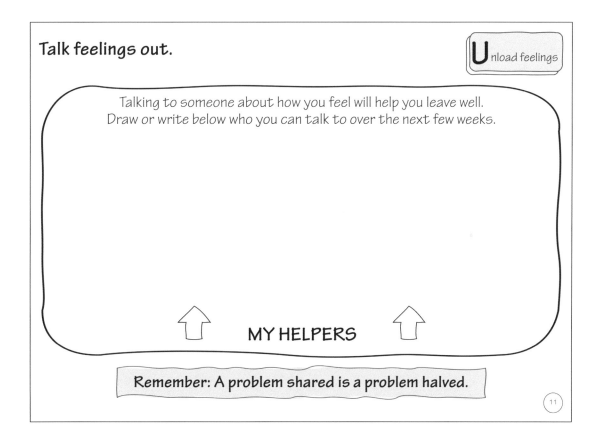

Materials needed: Each child needs: Pen, pencil, rubber, sharpener, coloured pens/pencils, activity book.

Setting the scene: You may say, *'Talking about how you feel helps to leave well. This page encourages you to think about who might be helpful to talk to about how you feel. These people are your "leaving well helpers"'.*

Completing the activity:

1) Invite the child/ren to close their eyes. Ask them to bring to mind people or even pets who are helpful to talk to about how they feel.

2) Ask the child/ren to open their eyes, look at the box on the page and draw or write down who they can talk to over the next few weeks in the box.

Facilitator's top tip: If the child/ren are having a hard time thinking of someone, you may ask them when the last time was they had a chat with someone and felt better. If they are still unable to think of someone you may ask, *'Suppose there was someone you could talk to, who might that be?'* If they are still stuck, ask the child/ren to draw colours shapes, lines, and squiggles in their box to represent being listened to.

3) You may say, *'Talking feelings out can help you feel better, it releases them, so they are not stuck inside you'*. You may ask, *'Would you be willing to share a time when you talked about how you felt with someone, and it helped?'* Invite responses.

4) Ask the child/ren to share as little or as much as they would like about their page with you or in a group setting, the person next to them.

5) Ask the child/ren to turn to page 12 and add another box. Invite them to write inside it: 'Talking to a helper about how I feel'.

Closure: You may say, *'I appreciate you thinking carefully about this page. Remember that a problem shared is problem halved and talking about how you feel helps to leave well'*.

Extension activity: Invite the child/ren to choose one of their helpers. Ask: *'What would this person say to reassure (help you feel better) about the move?* You may like to invite the child/ren to add the reassuring comment to their page, tell you or a partner, or just think about it for themselves.

*****

Leaving Well Activity Book

Page title: And there's more.

Page no: 12

Page rationale: There are many ways you can express how you feel. The more creative you get, the better. Everyone is unique and will prefer different ways to express. This page offers a variety of options for unloading feelings and helps the child/ren to acknowledge their preferred ways of taking good care of their feelings.

Page visual:

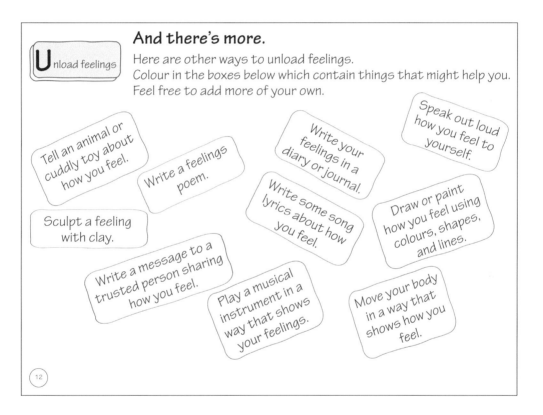

Materials needed: Each child needs: Pen, pencil, rubber, sharpener, coloured pens/pencils, activity book.

Setting the scene: You may say, *'This page helps to think of creative ways to unload feelings. Remember, we are all unique and what we find helpful differs from person to person. It's good to know what your preferred way of taking care of your feelings is, so you can be ready when big feelings arrive'.*

Completing the activity:

1) You may say: *'Have a look at the boxes on this page They offer some ideas of how to take good care of your feelings. Take some time to read through them now'*. Or you may like to read them aloud yourself.

2) Next, invite the child/ren to colour in boxes they find helpful, or might find helpful.

3) Invite the child/ren to add one or more boxes showing what helps them unload feelings or something they would like to try that's not on the page.

Closure: You may say: *'There are so many ways you can unload feelings, do pay attention to times when you manage to use one of these strategies and it helps you feel better. When this happens congratulate yourself for taking good care of your feelings. If you are feeling stressed, try coming back to this page to look for ideas of how to help yourself'*.

Extension activity: You may like to ask the child/ren to choose their top three strategies and rank them 1–3, with 1 being the most helpful. Find a way for them to share their top 3. They can share this with you, their partner or you may invite popcorn responses; the children speak out their answers in random order.

*****

Leaving Well Activity Book

Page title: Hope and fears flower.

Page no: 13

Page rationale: Being able to articulate hopes and fears about the move brings balance. It's helpful to be realistic; with every transition, there are pros and cons. This page helps to normalise and validate hopes and fears; it also fosters an appreciation that these are unique to everyone and every situation.

Page visual:

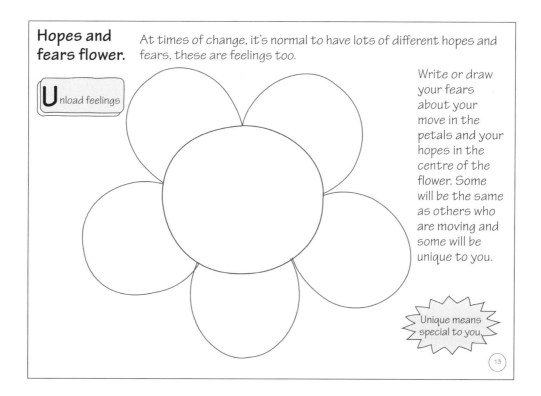

Materials needed: Each child needs: Pen, pencil, rubber, sharpener, coloured pens/pencils, activity book, spare paper as needed, example page of other children's answers (included below).

Setting the scene: You may say, *'At times of change, it's normal to feel hopeful and fearful; being aware of this and unloading feelings by sharing them helps to keep balanced and steady'.*

Facilitator's top tip: If they've forgotten what transition means, you may say, *'Transition means moving from one thing to another, in your case, one country to another'*.

Completing the activity:

1) You may say, *'This page has a flower on it; this is your hopes and fears flower. Let's think first about fears, the worries you have about the move, these are unique to everyone, but we'll probably find that lots of us have similar fears. Write five fears you have, one in each of the petals'*.

Facilitator's top tip: If the child/ren ask you what unique means, direct their attention to the grey star, bottom right of the page.

Facilitator's top tip: If the child/ren can't think of any fears, let them know that most children's fears are centred around leaving their friends and making new ones; you may ask them if that is true for them. If you are a parent supporting your child with their activity book, do share your developmentally appropraite fears.

2) After the child/ren have added their fears in the petals, invite sharing of what they have written with you or, in a group setting, with a partner. If you are working with a group you may like to ask each child to share a fear one by one or invite a popcorn response; the children speak their fear out loud in random order.
3) You may say, *'Thank you for sharing your fears about the move, that's not an easy thing to do, but remember, as we have learnt, telling others how we feel helps us to cope better at times of change'*.
4) Next, move onto the hopes. Invite the child/ren to add these to the centre of the flower. Encourage the child/ren to share with you or the group. If you are a parent supporting your child with their activity book, do share your hopes.

Facilitator's top tip: In a larger group, you may consider another way to share; get two buckets or boxes, one labelled 'hopes'and the other 'fears'. Invite the children to write one hope and one fear on paper, and place them in the respective bucket or box. Once they have done this, you may pull out a few and read them. This serves as a good way to show similarities and differences between everyone's hopes and fears.

5) You may like to share this example, the next page, of responses from other children. You may invite reflection by asking, *'Are the hopes and fears different or quite like yours?'*

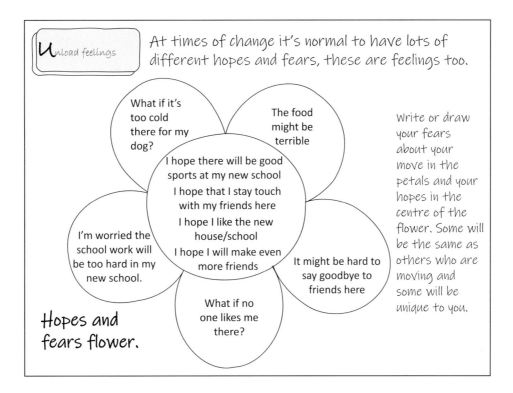

At times of change it's normal to have lots of different hopes and fears, these are feelings too.

Unload feelings

What if it's too cold there for my dog?

The food might be terrible

I hope there will be good sports at my new school
I hope that I stay touch with my friends here
I hope I like the new house/school
I hope I will make even more friends

I'm worried the school work will be too hard in my new school.

It might be hard to say goodbye to friends here

What if no one likes me there?

Hopes and fears flower.

Write or draw your fears about your move in the petals and your hopes in the centre of the flower. Some will be the same as others who are moving and some will be unique to you.

Closure: Thank the child/ren for creating their flowers; let them know they can come back to this page to add hopes and fears as they continue their 'moving on' journey.

Extension activity: If appropriate, in a school/therapy setting, you may like to encourage the child/ren to share their hopes and fears flowers with an adult at home and talk to them about their flower. Consider letting the parents/guardians know the plan.

*****

Leaving Well Activity Book

Page title: Who and how?

Page no: 14

Page rationale: This page encourages the child to think about who has made a difference in their time in their current place and make plans to say thank you. Listing the WHO and HOW of saying thank you increases the chances of following through and reduces the risk of forgetting someone. Saying thank you helps to bring closure; acknowledging those special people is an important part of leaving well. Affirmations help others feel appreciated and boost the wellbeing of the person saying thanks.

Page visual:

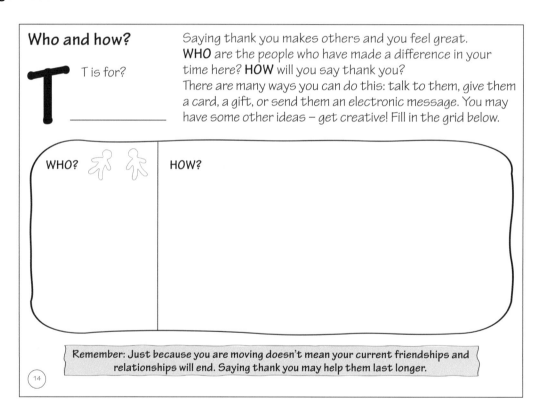

Materials needed: Each child needs: Pen, pencil, rubber, sharpener, coloured pens/pencils, activity book, spare paper as needed.

Setting the scene: You may say, *'Saying thank you is an important part of leaving well. It helps not only the person you are thanking, but yourself as well. We are going to carefully make a list of all the people you'd like to thank so you don't forget anyone'.*

Completing the activity:

1) Begin by inviting the child/ren to fill in the **T is for** _____ on their page. You may say, *'Now, we move onto the third letter of GUTS[2]. Can you remember what T stands for?'* (Elicit from the child/ren: Thank you).

2) You may say, *'We are going to begin with the column on the left of your page that says WHO? Let's think about different groups of people you may like to thank. First, let's think about friends at school, these could be in your class, on your bus, or you may know them from clubs at school'*. Invite the child/ren to write down anything that comes to mind in the WHO? column.

3) Next, ask the child/ren to think of any adults at school, teachers, coaches, support staff that they'd like to thank and add them to the WHO? column.

4) After that, ask the child/ren if they are leaving behind any family members they'd like to thank. Invite them to add these as necessary to the WHO? column.

5) Next, invite the child to think about their community, friends/adults in their neighbourhood, team-mates/coaches from sports teams or other clubs/lessons and add anyone to thank from this group to the WHO? column.

6) Check in with the child/ren to see if there is anyone not included in their WHO? column they'd like to add. You might say *'Have a look at your list, did we forget anyone?'*

7) Next move onto the HOW? column, on the right. You may say, *'We've carefully thought about who to thank, now we'll think about how you can do this. Let's move over to the HOW? column'*.

8) If you are supporting one child, guide them through each person in their WHO? column, inviting them to think about how they may say thanks and ask them to record this in their HOW? column. There are lots of options here; for some of their chosen people, they might simply say thank you; for others, they might write a card, electronic message, or even give a gift. In a larger group, the children will need to be more independent with this part of the exercise. Feel free to give examples of these options and ask for their ideas on how to say thanks too.

Facilitator's top tip: Have some spare paper ready as some child/ren's list may be quite long.

Closure: You may say, *'We've been thinking a lot about saying thank you, haven't we? I'd like to thank YOU for thinking so carefully about this important part of leaving well. This page can act as a checklist, you'll still need to decide the best time and place to say thank you to the people you have identified. At the bottom of your page, in the grey box, it says something important, have a look at your page now; it says, "Remember: just because you are moving doesn't mean that your current friendships and relationships will end. Saying thank you may help them last longer"'*.

*****

Leaving Well Activity Book

Page title: Staying connected.

Page no: 15

Page rationale: Staying in contact with people where you moved from increases the longevity of important relationships. Gathering contact information makes it clear to both parties that the intention is to maintain contact. Having the contact information to hand during and after the move increases the chances of staying connected.

Page visual:

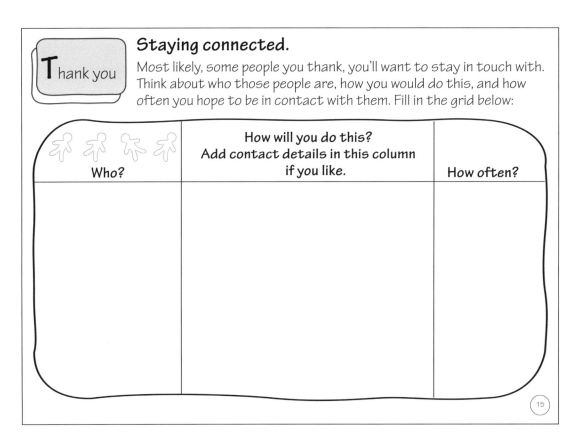

Materials needed: Each child needs: Pen, pencil, rubber, sharpener, coloured pens/pencils, activity book, spare paper as needed.

Setting the scene: You may say, '*Most likely, there are people who you thought of saying thanks to, whose contact details you would like to take with you. Having their details on this page, in one place, increases the chances of you staying connected*'.

Completing the activity:

1) You may say, *'This is a page I'm going to ask you to complete mostly in your own time. For now, I'm going to ask you to think of the top three people you would like to stay in touch with and write their names in the left hand* Who? *column. Write those first three names now'.*

2) Ask the child/ren to consider their first person, move to the 'How will you do this?' column, ask them to write how they plan to stay connected, adding contact details if they know them; if they don't, they can add them at another time.

3) Staying with the first person, ask the child/ren to move across to the last column and write how often they hope to be in touch.

4) Ask the child/ren to repeat this for persons 2 and 3.

5) Let the child/ren know that you encourage them to continue filling in this page in their own time.

Closure: Let the child/ren know, if their list is too long for the page, they are welcome to extend the list onto some extra paper. You may like to provide this for them. You may say, *'Staying in touch with key people is a big part of leaving and arriving well, remember it's important to find a balance of the old and the new'.*

*****

Leaving Well Activity Book

Page title: What brings me joy?

Page no: 16

Page rationale: Self-care is an important part of wellbeing, especially at times of transition. Change gets busy. This page helps the child/ren acknowledge what activities give them a wellbeing boost and encourages them to intentionally engage in these to leave well.

Page visual:

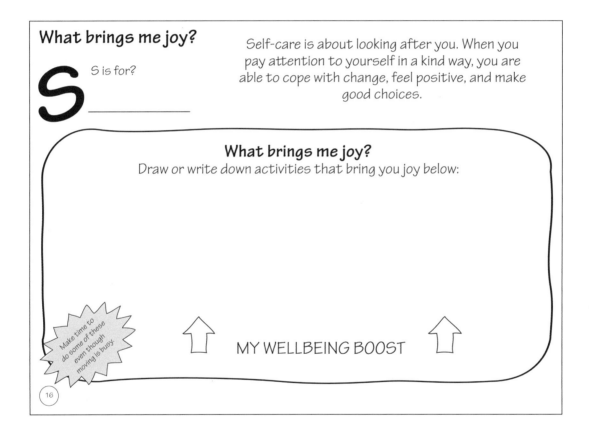

Materials needed: Each child needs: Pen, pencil, rubber, sharpener, coloured pens/pencils, activity book.

Setting the scene: You may say, *'When we are moving it's such a busy time. It's easy to forget about looking after yourself but doing so helps you be able to cope with busyness. The next few pages look at self-care which is how you look after you'.*

Completing the activity:

1) Begin by inviting the child/ren to fill in the blank, **S is for** _____ on their page. You may say, *'Now, we move to the fourth letter of GUTS[2]. Can you remember what the S stands for?'* (Elicit from the child/ren: Self-care).

2) You may say, *'This page is unique to you, no two pages will look the same. Think about things you do you enjoy, examples might include doing something sporty, something in nature, something artistic, writing, talking with someone, or something musical. What do you love to do? Write or draw these things in the box on this page'.*

3) Find a way for the child/ren to share something from their page. You may like to do this verbally or in a charades type activity, asking the child/ren to mime something from their page for you or others to guess the activity.

Facilitator's top tip: If you are in a group setting and some children finish before others, ask those who have finished to rank the things they have written or drawn on their page in terms of enjoyment. 1 being the most enjoyable.

Closure: You may say, *'Moving is such a busy time, it's easy to do less of the things you enjoy. However, it's important for your self-care to still make time for them. Remember, the better you look after you, the more likely you will leave well'.*

*****

Leaving Well Activity Book

Page title: What does my body tell me?

Page no: 17

Page rationale: This page develops interoception. Interoception is the ability to sense signals from the body. When interoception is honed, our ability to answer the question 'how do I feel?' at any given moment is increased. Kelly Mahler, a world-renowned occupational therapist, says that interoception has a huge influence on many areas of our lives like self-regulation, mental health, and social connection. This page helps the child get familiar with their 'Stress Signature'.

Page visual:

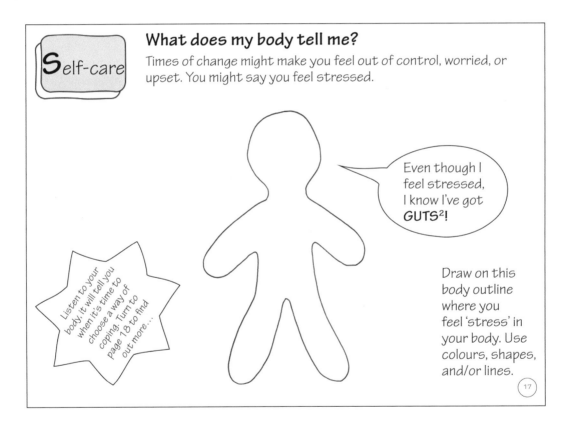

Materials needed: Each child needs: Pen, pencil, rubber, sharpener, coloured pens/pencils, activity book.

Setting the scene: You may say, *'Your body will tell you when you feel stressed. Listening to signals your body gives you helps be in control of big emotions'.*

Completing the activity:

1) You may say, *'Everyone feels stress in their body differently. Think about how your body tells you you're feeling stressed. Can you give me some examples?'* Talk through a few examples and how the child/ren might draw this on their body outline. For example, they may say, 'my heart beats faster', you may say, *'Yes, that's a great example, how would you draw that on your body outline?'* Other examples may include a feeling of butterflies in their tummy, breathing faster, fidgety hands and feet, clenched hands, sweating, going red in the face, tears in their eyes, and/or a 'fuzzy' head.

2) Invite the child/ren to add colours, shapes, lines, and/or squiggles to the inside of their body outline to show what they feel in their body when stress arrives. They may also want to add annotations.

3) Find the most appropriate way for the child/ren to share what they have drawn of written on their body outlines.

Closure: You may say, *'Before we meet again, your job is to notice when your body lets you know you feel stressed. As you get curious about this, you may notice there are other ways your body lets you know this; feel free to add these to this page too. Next, we'll look at page 18 which gives you some ideas to steady yourself when you notice your body giving you a sign'.*

*****

Leaving Well Activity Book

Page title: How do I cope well?

Page no: 18

Page rationale: Identifying coping strategies ahead of time boosts resilience. Having coping strategies at the ready can help make a good choice in moments of overwhelm. However, 'one size doesn't fit all'; everyone is unique and finds different things helpful. This page offers a variety of options that span a diverse range of coping strategies.

Page visual:

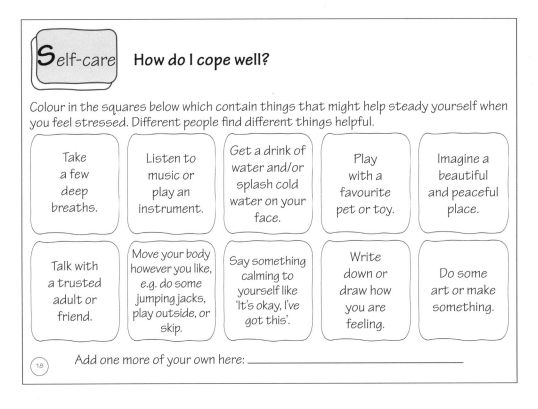

Materials needed: Each child needs: Pen, pencil, rubber, sharpener, coloured pens/pencils, activity book.

Setting the scene: You may say, *'When you notice your body signal that big emotions have arrived, it gives you the chance to choose a way of coping. Everyone is unique and will have different ways of coping that work best for them'*.

Completing the activity:

1) Bring the child/ren's attention to the 10 boxes on this page. Choose the most appropriate way for them to read or be lead through each of the boxes. For each box you may ask, *'Have you (or who has) tried this one and found it helpful?'* You may also like to ask, *'Have you (or who has) not tried this one but think it might help?'*

2) Invite the child/ren to colour in the boxes which they think would be the best coping strategies for them.

3) Ask them if they'd like to write one of their own on the line provided at the bottom of the page.

Facilitator's top tip: If you are in a group setting and some children finish this before others, ask those who have finished to rank the coping strategies in terms preference. 1 being the most helpful.

Closure: You may say, *'Thank you for thinking about your favourite ways of coping. Do try some of these out, see if it's possible to notice your body telling you that you feel stressed and make a choice to use one of your ways of coping to steady yourself'.*

Extension activity: If time allows, you may lead the 'Safe space visualisation' below. It supports the top-right hand strategy on the page, 'Imagine a beautiful and peaceful place'.

Safe space visualisation:

The script below is designed to lead the child/ren whilst they are seated on a chair. Feel free to adjust the script if the child/ren are in a different position.

'Get yourself comfortable in your seat, adjust your body position a little if you need to.
Begin by closing your eyes if that feels comfortable.
As you sit here, notice your feet in contact with the floor.
Be aware of your body sitting in the chair, notice which bits of your body are in contact with the chair, notice which parts of your body are not.
Be aware of the air around you, notice if it's warm or cold, moving or still.
Now, notice your breathing, no need to change your breathing, notice the inbreath and the outbreath. Breathing in and breathing out. Notice how your body rises on the inbreath and falls on the outbreath.
Now, bringing to mind a peaceful, beautiful place. A place where you feel safe and peaceful. This could be a place you know well. It could be a place you have seen in a photograph, or it could even be an imaginary place.

Allow the image of this place to become clearer in your mind. (Pause).

Imagine you are in this safe place. I am going to invite you now, to explore this special place using your senses:

Firstly, notice what you can see in this safe place, take in as much detail as you can, notice colours, lines, shapes, objects, there may be people, animals, buildings, trees, or water. Take a moment to look down at your clothes and shoes, notice what you are wearing. (Pause).

Notice what you can see close to, and far away in your peaceful place. (Pause).

Next, using your sense of hearing, notice what can be heard in your safe place, it could be sounds of animals, the weather, the ocean, city sounds, music, or people talking. Tune into the sounds you can hear. (Pause).

Now, using your sense of touch. Notice what is here to be felt in your peaceful place. Feel whatever you are sitting on, or if you are standing or lying down sensing into what it feels like to be in contact with whatever is underneath you. You may be able to feel the touch of your clothes on your skin or the air around you. You may like to move around your safe place now or reach out to touch objects that call for your attention. (Pause).

Moving to the sense of smell, now. Take a long, deep breath, breathe in the energy this place gives you and breathe out again. On the next deep inbreath notice what is in your peaceful place to be smelled. (Pause).

Lastly, tune into your sense of taste. What can you taste in your safe place? It might be something that you are eating or have eaten in this place. It might be a favourite taste.

You might like to spend a little longer connecting with your beautiful, peaceful place noticing whatever calls for your attention. (Pause).

Letting your safe, peaceful place go now. Knowing that you can come back here anytime you need to.

Becoming aware of your breathing again, your inbreath and outbreath. Breathing in and breathing out, your body rising and falling. (Pause).

Becoming aware again of your body sitting in the chair, the parts in contact with the chair and those not.

Notice your feet in contact with the floor.

Now, open your eyes, come back into this room'.

Facilitator's top tip: As a closure and integration activity, you may ask the children to describe their safe place. If time allows, you may invite the children to draw their safe place and share as appropriate.

*****

Leaving Well Activity Book

Page title: What encouraging things can I say to myself?

Page no: 19

Page rationale: Our 'inner critic' gets more active at times of change. Being aware of thoughts helps us resist getting swept away by them. Our internal dialogue impacts how we feel and act. This page mobilises the child's 'inner coach' – shifting the internal narrative to encouraging statements helps in times of change.

Page visual:

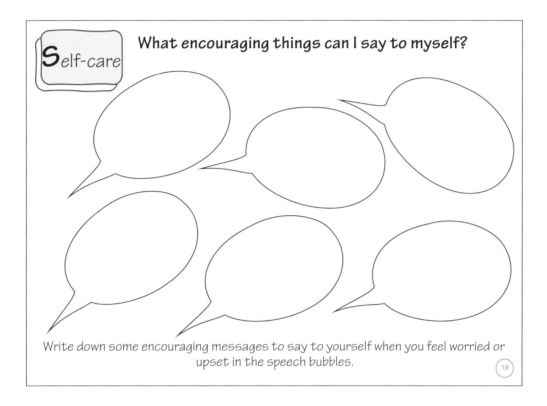

Materials needed: Each child needs: Pen, pencil, rubber, sharpener, coloured pens/pencils, activity book.

Setting the scene: You may say, '*How you speak to yourself impacts how you feel and what you do. You can choose to say kind, encouraging things that help you feel better when you are worried, upset, or need to find courage. This page helps you think about what you can say to yourself in times of need*'.

Completing the activity:

1) You may say, *'You have thoughts coming and going all the time. At times of change, like now, you'll get even more. Sometimes you'll be aware of them, sometimes not. Sometimes the thoughts are unkind, these sorts of thoughts don't make you feel good. I'm going to ask you to think of some kind messages you can tell yourself to cope well when things are tough'.*

2) You may say, *'Take your time to write down six encouraging, kind messages you'd like to hear when you need a bit of extra encouragement. Add one to each speech bubble'.*

3) Give the child/ren time to write their messages down.

4) You may like to invite sharing of one or more of their messages. If you are working with one child, you may like to get them to read one or more of their messages aloud to you. In a group setting, you may like to get the children moving around the room sharing their messages of encouragement with each other.

Facilitator's top tip: If the child/ren find it difficult to think of statements, ask them to think of a helpful person in their life. Ask them what that person would say to encourage them to cope when things are tough.

Closure: You may say, *'The more you say these messages to yourself, the easier they will be to recall at times of challenge – in your own time practice saying them to yourself.*

Thank you for thinking about how you speak to yourself, this is an important piece not only of leaving well but for life in general'.

Extension activity: You might like to invite the child/ren to write their messages on post-it notes and put them up somewhere helpful for them. Another suggestion may be to write one or more messages on their bathroom or bedroom mirror with a glass marker, so that they will see the message/s daily.

*****

Leaving Well Activity Book

Page title: What's in and out of my control?

Page no: 20

Page rationale: This page helps to understand what can and can't be controlled. Trying to take charge of things outside of one's control can leave people feeling anxious, overwhelmed, unable to cope well. This negatively impacts wellbeing.

Page visual:

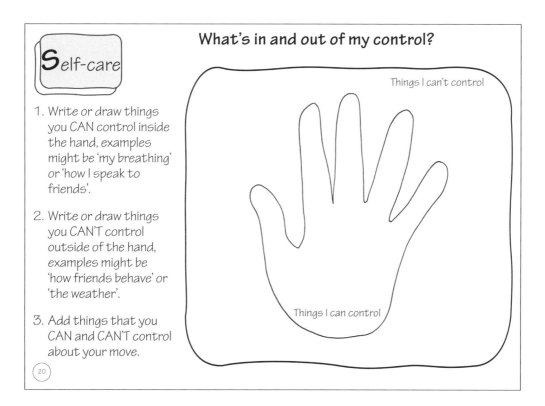

Materials needed: Each child needs: Pen, pencil, rubber, sharpener, coloured pens/pencils, activity book.

Setting the scene: You may say, '*At times of change, things can feel out of control. If you spend time trying to influence things that are not in your control, it can make you feel anxious and upset. Making a choice to focus on what you can control helps you to cope better with transition*'.

Completing the activity:

1) You may say, *'The hand exercise on this page will help you understand things you can control and things you can't'.*

2) Guide the child/ren through each of the steps by reading through 1, 2, and 3 on the left of the page. As you do this, you might like to gather examples from the child/ren, in addition to those listed on the page.

3) If time permits, offer the 'What I can control exercise', below which asks the child/ren to count five things in their control on the fingers of one hand. Ask them to use their index finger on their other hand to touch each finger as they do this. This exercise can be done silently or aloud. Get them to take a big, deep breath at the beginning and end. Encourage them to start each example with 'I can control….':

What I can control exercise:

    ~Deep breath
  'I can control *my feelings'*.
  'I can control *my thoughts'*.
  'I can control *what I do'*.
  'I can control *what I say'*.
  'I can control *my breathing'*.
    ~Deep Breath~

Closure: You may say, *'It's helpful to remember; "If it's in your hands you can control it, if not let it go". If you feel overwhelmed by something, count five things on your hands that you can control. Don't forget your two big, deep breaths at the beginning and end'.*

Extension activity: You may like to try this pipe cleaner and pebble activity:

1) Give each child a pipe cleaner, time 2 minutes in which they are invited to create something with it.

2) Get the child/ren to share what they have made.

3) You might say *'Great creativity, you changed the pipe cleaner into something, you had control of it, is that right?'*

4) Ask the students to place their pipe cleaner creation to one side.

5) Next, give the child/ren a pebble, rock, or marble. Ask them to create the same thing with the rock that they created with the pipe cleaner. They will most likely respond with 'what?', 'huh?', 'I can't!'. Ask them to explain what's different about this challenge.

6) You may say, *'You can't change the rock. You don't have control over what shape it is. Some problems are like the pipe cleaners – we have control over them and can change them. Some problems are like rocks – we don't have control over them'.*

7) Collect in the pipe cleaner and rocks or allow the child/ren to keep hold of them to remind them about what they learned in this exercise.

*****

Leaving Well Activity Book

Page title: Mindful colouring.

Page no: 21

Page rationale: Many children (and adults!) find mindful colouring relaxing. Mindful colouring can be a regulatory strategy. Some people rarely feel calm, they may need to re-teach their bodies and minds to be able to settle in a relaxed state; mindful colouring is one way to do this. The more often we engage in relaxing activities, the better we get at finding moments of calm.

Page visual:

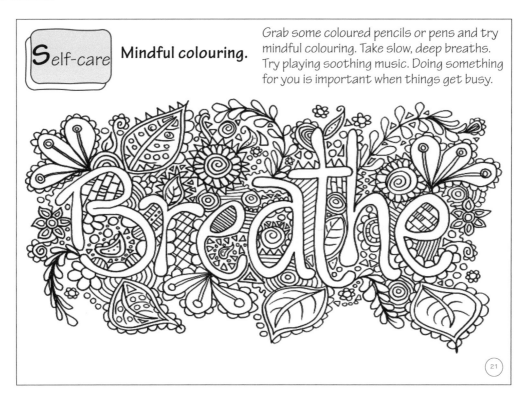

Self-care Mindful colouring.

Grab some coloured pencils or pens and try mindful colouring. Take slow, deep breaths. Try playing soothing music. Doing something for you is important when things get busy.

21

Materials needed: Each child needs: Pen, pencil, rubber, sharpener, a variety of coloured pens/pencils, activity book. Optional: Soothing music, timer.

Setting the scene: You may say, *'When you are mindful, you choose where to place your attention. Mindful colouring helps take care of your mind as you are choosing to place your attention on something creative. When you do this, your mind rests in the present, rather than worrying about what's going to happen or has happened. Mindful colouring helps your body to relax too'.*

Completing the activity:

1) Before the child/ren begin, you may ask them to choose one word to describe how their mind and body feels – give an example of your own, *e.g. 'My mind feels busy; my body feels heavy'*. There is no right or wrong. Challenge the child/ren to stick to one word.

2) Once they have begun colouring you may say: *'As you colour, notice your feet flat on the floor, give your feet a little wiggle if you like. As you keep colouring, notice your breathing, be aware you are breathing in and out. You might like to make the in-breath and the out-breath slightly longer'*.

Facilitator's top tip: Have a variety of different pens and pencils accessible so that the child/ren stay seated whilst colouring.

Facilitator's top tip: You might like to show the class/child an example of a completed page so they can see how their page may look.

Facilitator's top tip: The children will progress with this page at different rates; you might like to set a timer.

Facilitator's top tip: Playing relaxing music whilst the child/ren engage with their mindful colouring helps to create a calm atmosphere.

3) At the end of your mindful colouring time, repeat 1) above. You might like to reflect on their answers by highlighting (if appropriate); *'Isn't it curious how mindful colouring has made a difference to your body and mind?'*

Closure: You may say: *'Every time you practice mindful colouring, you are reminding your body and mind how to relax. You might like to try this as activity when you notice stress showing up in your body to help steady yourself. Thanks for being creative today'*.

Extension activity: To encourage reflection, you may ask *'What did you discover during the activity?'* Invite discussion, either with you, in pairs, or whole group sharing.

*****

Leaving Well Activity Book

Page title: Take 5.

Page no: 22

Page rationale: Take 5 is a way to regulate breathing. Regulated breathing helps the mind and body to relax. Take 5 is a handy (!) strategy to include in a self-regulation toolbox.

Page visual:

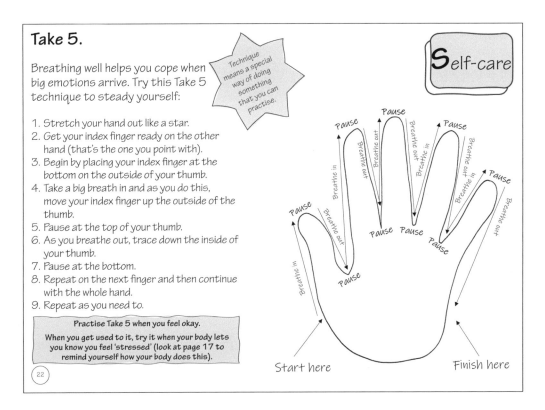

Materials needed: Each child needs: Pen, pencil, rubber, sharpener, coloured pens/pencils, activity book.

Setting the scene: You may say, *'We are going to learn a breathing technique you can try when you feel stress in your body. Technique means a special way of doing something you can practise. It's called Take 5, it will help you slow down your breathing, think more clearly and make good decisions'.*

Completing the activity:

1) Before the child/ren begin, you may ask them to choose one word to describe how their mind and body feels – give an example of your own, *e.g. 'My mind feels busy; my body feels heavy'*. There is no right or wrong. Challenge the child/ren to stick to one word.
2) Ask the child/ren to get themselves comfortable. They might need to adjust their position a little.
3) Guide them through the instructions for Take 5 on the page.
4) At the end of Take 5, repeat 1) above. You might like to reflect on their answers by highlighting (if appropriate), *'Take 5 has helped your body and mind relax'*.

Facilitator's top tip: Asking the child/ren to choose their favourite hand when they stretch it out like a star can add a little humour to this activity.

Facilitator's top tip: You may choose to begin your next session with Take 5, creating a link between one session and the next.

Closure: Bring the child/ren's attention to the grey box at the bottom of the page. Encourage them to practise their Take 5 when they feel okay to be able to use it when feeling overwhelmed. You may give them a challenge to practise Take 5 every day until you meet again.

Extension activity: To help the child/ren stay connected to Take 5, you might encourage them to teach this skill to someone else and to report back next time you meet.

*****

Leaving Well Activity Book

Page title: Thankfulness tree.

Page no: 23

Page rationale: Martin Seligman, world-renowned psychologist, states that cultivating an 'attitude of gratitude' positively impacts wellbeing. What we pay attention to grows; when we are intentionally thankful, we notice more of the good. Making this a regular practice such as the one included on this page lifts mood.

Page visual:

Materials needed: Each child needs: Pen, pencil, rubber, sharpener, coloured pens/pencils, activity book. Optional: Thankful exercise cards to instructions to take away.

Setting the scene: You may say, *'Today we are going to practise being thankful. Being thankful helps notice the good and gives a wellbeing boost'.*

Completing the activity:

1) You may say, *'Let's begin by thinking of a few things you are thankful for. These can be big things like your family or school and they can be everyday things like drinking a nice glass of water or cuddling your pet'.* If you are supporting one child, brainstorm some ideas (do share examples of your own too). If you are in a group setting, find a way to gather ideas from group.

Facilitator's top tip: You may consider setting a timer for one minute and inviting the child/ren to write down as many things they are thankful for as they can. In a group setting, invite sharing of things the children added to their lists.

2) Once you have some examples, ask the child/ren to begin populating their thankfulness tree by writing or drawing one thing they are thankful for on each leaf.

Facilitator's Top tip: Highlight that each tree will be unique as everyone is different and are thankful for different things.

Facilitator's Top tip: If you are in a group setting, some children may finish before others. Invite those who have completed their tree to add colour to their page, making their tree unique.

3) Next, bring the child/ren's attention to the grey star at the bottom left of the page. Guide them through the activity by reading it aloud. If you are supporting a group, you may like to get them to speak the sentence in unison, 'I am thankful for (they add whatever they have on their leaf)'. Get the children to close their eyes for the next part of the activity. Invite them to take a deep breath in unison. Repeat this for the remaining nine leaves.

Closure: You may say, *'Noticing what you feel thankful for everyday lifts mood, which helps you deal better with change'.* If you are a parent supporting your child, you may say, *'Come back to this page at a time that suits you every day for a week and do the exercise in the grey star again. I'd be so interested to hear how it's helpful'.* If you are in a school/therapy setting, you may like to say the same if the child/ren take the activity books home. If not, you may say, *'You might like to continue being thankful until we meet again. If so, you might notice three things you are thankful for every* *night before bed or when you get up in the morning. I'd be interested to know how you get on'.* Feel free to copy and share the 'Thankfulness exercise' instructions below as a reminder:

Thankfulness exercise:

Thankfulness Exercise

1) Think of something you are thankful for.
2) Say out loud; "I am thankful for... (say what it is)."
3) Close your eyes and bring to mind whatever it is.
4) Take a big breath in through your nose and out through your mouth.
5) Repeat 1) – 4) with two more things you're thankful for.

*****

Leaving Well Activity Book

Page title: Stand like a tree.

Page no: 24

Page rationale: 'Stand like a tree' is a practice that can be called upon to ground oneself. It's a mindful activity that promotes understanding that feelings of chaos are temporary, and being strong and grounded helps manage difficult moments. The movement in this activity helps shift internal physiology to a positive state.

Page visual:

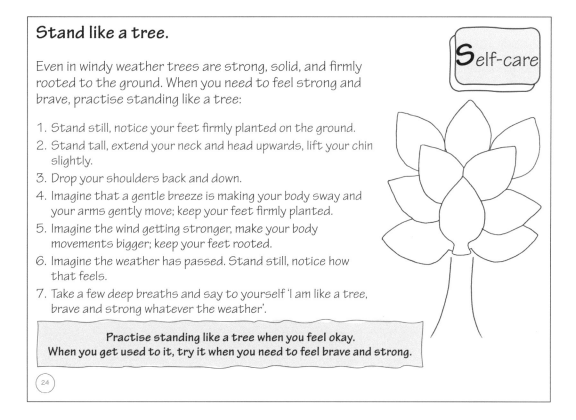

Materials needed: Each child needs: Their activity book. Optional: Spare paper or body outline (the body outline can be copied from page 57).

Setting the scene: You may say, '*This page shows you a way to be mindful When you are mindful, you choose where to place your attention in the present moment. You* *are going to pretend to be a tree. Even in windy weather, trees are strong, solid, firmly rooted to the ground. This is a great exercise to try when you need to feel strong and brave'.*

Facilitator's top tip: The child/ren may ask you, 'What is the present moment?' You may say, *'The present moment is right now, not in the past or the future. For example, can you pay attention what you can hear now?'* Get them to do this briefly. You may say, *'When you do this, you are placing your attention on sounds that are happening in this present moment'.*

Completing the activity:

1) Ensure the child/ren have enough space so they won't hit any objects or other children around them. Get them to practise swinging their arms to make sure they are in a good spot before you begin.
2) Lead the activity, slowly moving through the steps on the page.
3) Ask the child/ren what they can learn through this exercise. You might say, *'At the end of the exercise, I asked you to say to yourself "I am like a tree, brave and strong whatever the weather". What does it teach us about change?'* Hopefully they will share, difficult times don't last forever, challenges come and go like the weather. They may say that even though, we feel stressed sometimes, we can cope by staying steady, strong, and grounded. If they are not forthcoming, you might say, *'We might think of this time of change as a bit like the weather, it will not last forever If you can stay strong and steady like a tree, you can get through it, as best you can'.*

Facilitator's top tip: If time and location allow, you may do this exercise outside in a natural setting.

Closure: You may say, *'It's important to practise standing like a tree when you feel okay. When you get used to it, try it at a time you need to be brave and strong'.*

Extension activity: If time allows, get the child/ren to draw a body outline or have one drawn already; you may like to copy the body outline on page 57 for this purpose.

Invite the child/ren to draw colours, shapes, lines, and/or squiggles on their body outline to show how their body felt when they were standing tall and strong as a tree.

Body outline:

*****

Leaving Well Activity Book

Page title: Get curious.

Page no: 25

Page rationale: This page invites the child/ren to build their curiosity by 'saying hello' to their next place. Awakening curiosity increases capacity to cope with change by fostering psychological flexibility. According to neurological studies, the more inquisitive a child gets, the more they are willing to learn, discover, and explore, which is directly translatable to the process of transition. This page and the next, draws on the adage that 'knowledge is power' – the more information the child/ren glean about where they are going, the more prepared and ready they'll feel.

Page visual:

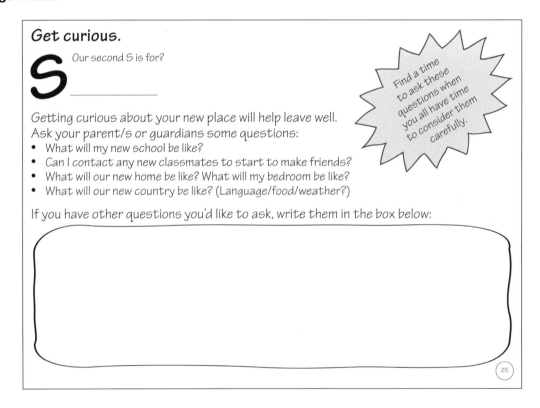

Materials needed: Each child needs: Pen, pencil, rubber, sharpener, coloured pens/pencils, activity book. Optional: Questions written on another piece or paper or plain scrap paper.

Setting the scene: You may say, *'It's time to "say hello" to where you are going. This, and the next three pages will awaken your curiosity about your next place. You'll get a better idea of where you are headed, which helps to leave well'.*

Completing the activity:

1) Begin by inviting the child/ren to fill in the blank, **S is for** _____ (Say hello). You may say, *'Now, we move onto the last letter of GUTS[2]. Can you remember what the second S stands for? (*Elicit from the child/ren: Say hello).

2) If you are the parent of the moving child, invite your child to ask you the questions on the page and any others that they can think of. You might not know all the answers; be honest about that and do your best to find out the answers together.

   If you are working with the child/ren in a school or therapy setting, you may say, *'This is a page to be completed in your own time. Find a time when it would be best to interview your parent/s or guardians. When do you think that might be?'* Gather responses. You may like to read through the questions with them; they may know the answers to some or all of them or they may not. Help them to think of additional questions they may ask to find out more.

Facilitator's top tip: If you are in a school or therapy setting, you may let the parent/s or guardians know their child has some important questions for them. Additionally, if you do not want the activity books to go home, have the questions typed up for the child/ren or get them to write them down.

Closure: If you are a parent or guardian, you may say, *'Thanks for asking me those questions. Your curiosity helped me to get a few things straight too'.* If you are in a school or therapy setting and the page is being completed outside of your session, you may say*, 'Good luck with finding the answers to your questions. I hope after using your curiosity in this way, next time you'll have the answers to these questions'.*

Extension activity: If you are in a school or therapy setting, you may like to ask the children to share the most interesting thing they found out at the start of your next session.

*****

Leaving Well Activity Book

Page title: Curiouser and curiouser…

Page no: 26

Page rationale: Curiosity opens the heart and mind to new opportunities. This page helps the child/ren to continue to 'say hello' to their new place by finding out more. By doing their own research, the child/ren take more ownership of the move which is empowering.

Page visual:

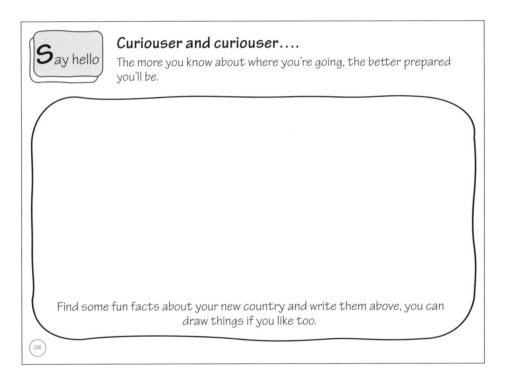

Materials needed: Each child needs: Pen, pencil, rubber, sharpener, coloured pens/pencils, activity book.

Setting the scene: You may say, *'We are going to continue being curious. This page invites you to find out fun facts about your new country. Remember, the more you know about where you are going, the better prepared you'll be'.*

Completing the activity:

1) Find out what the child/ren already know about their destination country and invite them to write or draw these things in the box on their page.

Facilitator's top tip: In a group setting, you may ask the children what they know about each other's destination countries. Invite the child/ren to add relevant facts that others share about where they are going to their page.

2) If you are a parent or guardian, you may choose to research together using the most appropriate sources. In a school or therapy setting, you may do the same or encourage more independent research. You may choose to set this task to be done outside of your session, either independently or with parents or guardians.

Facilitator's top tip: If you are in a school or therapy setting and you have asked the child/ren to complete this page in their own time, you may like to let the parent/s or guardians know their child has some important research to be done which they might need help with.

3) If you have supported the child/ren with populating their page, you may invite sharing of their favourite fun facts.

Closure: You may say, *'Thank you, I have learned so much about your (our) next country. "Saying hello" and being curious about the next stop has turned out to be a whole heap of fun'*. You may choose to share some of the most interesting fun facts you learned while the child/ren were completing this page.

Extension activity: If you are in a school or therapy setting and have asked the child/ren to complete their page in their own time, you may ask them to share the most interesting thing they found out at the start of your next session.

*****

Leaving Well Activity Book

Page title: Ballooning around.

Page no: 27

Page rationale: This page acknowledges the importance of bringing balance through realistic expectations of what life will be like in the next place. By identifying things they are looking forward to, the child/ren are drawing on their sense of hope. Naming things that might be a challenge helps to prepare and ready the child/ren to tackle things that may be tricky. If these challenges are matched with the ways to cope before they happen, the children feel capable and empowered to face transition challenges with resilience and confidence.

Page visual:

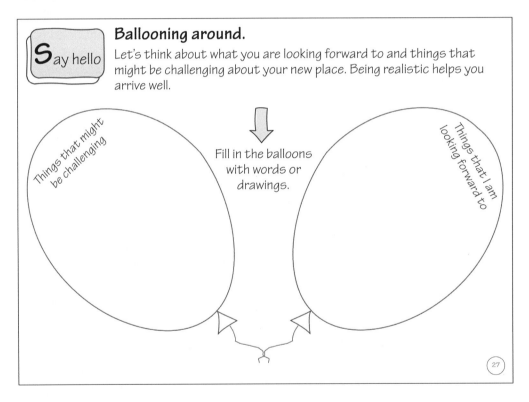

Materials needed: Each child needs: Pen, pencil, rubber, sharpener, coloured pens/pencils, activity book.

Setting the scene: You may say, *'An important part of "saying hello" is thinking about things you are looking forward to and acknowledging things you might find tricky. This helps to keep expectations in check. Being realistic helps arrive well'.*

Facilitator's top tip: If the child/ren ask what expectations are, you may say, *'Expectations are what we think might happen'.*

Completing the activity:

1) Let the child/ren know that this page is called 'Ballooning around' because there are two balloons on it – one to write things they are looking forward to in, and the other to write things that might be challenging.
2) Encourage them to begin with whichever balloon feels right, filling up one balloon and then the other with words or drawings.

Facilitator's top tip: Highlight that everyone's balloons are unique and special; no two balloons will be the same.

3) Find a way for the child/ren to share what's in their balloons.

Facilitator's top tip: In a group setting, some children will finish quicker than others. Encourage those who have competed the task to decorate their page in some way or return to page 21 to do some mindful colouring.

Closure: You may say, *'Well done, getting realistic is not always easy. There will be challenges for you in your new place but if you are ready for them, you'll be more able to cope. As you move on, remember the coping strategies that you've learnt in this activity book; they will help you to stay steady and strong in the face of challenge'.*

*****

Leaving Well Activity Book

Page title: Gallery of strengths.

Page no: 28

Page rationale: This page empowers the child/ren by helping them acknowledge character strengths they bring to their transition process. The activity brings the child/ren's strengths to life by acknowledging how their strengths are seen in action. Being able to notice and acknowledge strengths boosts self-esteem and self-efficacy with the ability to cope with change.

Page visual:

Materials needed: Each child needs: Pen, pencil, rubber, sharpener, coloured pens/pencils, activity book.

Setting the scene: You may say, *'We are going to get creative today, you will make your own, unique, art gallery. This is no ordinary art gallery; this is a gallery of strengths'.*

Completing the activity:

1) Read the left-hand side of the page to the child/ren. Ask them if they can think of some more strengths, you might like to record any additional ones somewhere in a place they can be seen as they complete their gallery.

2) Once you have read the bottom paragraph, ask them to draw their first strength in one of the boxes. You might like to give an example of a strength in action by saying, *'Drawing your strength in action means drawing how someone sees you demonstrating the strength, for example, if your strength is kindness, you might draw yourself helping someone carry something heavy, or if your strength is joyfulness, you might draw yourself singing'.*

Facilitator's top tip: Some children may find it difficult to acknowledge their strengths. If they are struggling, you might ask them to think of a friend or supportive adult and ask, *'What would that person say is brilliant about you?'* if they are still struggling, ask them, *'When was the last time you were with this person and having a good time? What strengths would that say they noticed you had in that moment.'* If they are still stumped, give them some examples of things that you have noticed in your time supporting them. You may even like to draw a strength of theirs you have noticed in one of their frames; invite the child to guess the strength in action you have drawn. When they have guessed correctly, ask them to write the strength on the line below the frame.

3) If you are supporting one child, you may like to playfully guess their strength in action they have drawn, before they write it on the line below the frame. This would also work in pairs in a group setting.
4) Ask the students to continue adding their strengths in action, writing them on the line underneath the frame, until they have finished their gallery.
5) Find a way for sharing strength galleries. If you are supporting one child, this may be with you; in a group setting, this may be with partners or if time permits, you may get the children moving around the room, creating an interactive gallery. Ask them to show their gallery to another group member, moving to another child when they are ready or on the sound of a bell. Another idea is to lay out all the galleries for the rest of the group to view.

Facilitator's top tip: If you are in a group setting, some children may finish before others. Ask those who have completed their gallery to draw a funky frame around each of their pictures like the one on the page.

Closure: You may say, *'Thank you for using your creativity today, I hope you included creativity as strength in your gallery. Remember you take your strengths with you wherever you go, they are what make you unique. Notice times that your strengths are in action and congratulate yourself for being the best version of you'.*

*****

Leaving Well Activity Book

Page title: Moving on poem.

Page no: 29

Page rationale: This page encourages the child to express their transition experience through the medium of poem. This can be a powerful experience, where the child gains perspective and groundedness. The parameters of length in this task help the child to consider carefully. The result is a poem that is representative of their lived experience through their transition thus far.

Page visual:

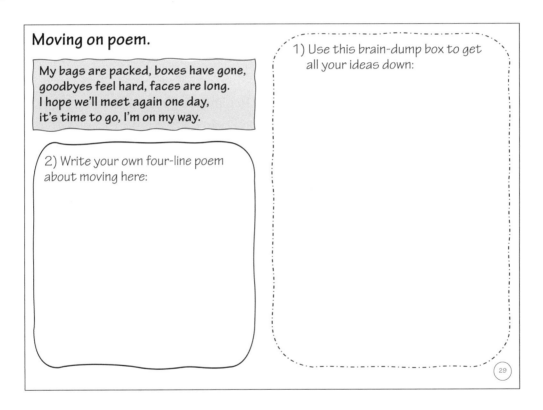

Materials needed: Each child needs: Pen, pencil, rubber, sharpener, coloured pens/pencils, activity book.

Setting the scene: You may say, *'This page invites you to get creative with your words to describe your experience of moving on so far'.*

Completing the activity:

1) Begin by reading through the poem at the top of the page. Highlight that the challenge of this task is to make a poem that is only four lines long.

2) Invite the child/ren to use the 'brain-dump' section on the right of the page to brainstorm feelings, things that have happened, what they have noticed in their body, thoughts, actions they or others have taken, things they have learned from their activity book, and anything else they feel it's important to include. This could be a list, a mind-map, and/or drawings.

3) Challenge the child/ren to choose the most important points, perhaps by underlining these.

4) Challenge the child/ren to weave these most important points into their four-line poem.

5) Find the most appropriate way for the child/ren to share their poem, some will be keen, others may like to keep their poem private; use your judgement with this.

Facilitator's top tip: Some children will need more support than others, be aware in a group setting of who these children might be.

Facilitator's top tip: If some students finish quickly, they can help others with the task or decorate their page to enhance their poem.

Closure: You may say, *'Squeezing your moving on experience into four lines is a tough task. Here's a fun fact: A four-line poem is called a quatrain! Well done on using your creativity to craft your very own quatrain'.*

Extension activity: If you are supporting a group, you may like to host a poetry recital, with poems being presented one at a time. Or you may get the children moving around the room, creating an interactive recital, sharing their quatrain out loud and moving to another child when they are ready or on your signal.

Another idea is to lay out the poems for the rest of the group to view.

*****

Leaving Well Activity Book

Page title: Moving on podium.

Page no: 30

Page rationale: This closure and integration activity helps the children reflect on what stood out for them from the *Leaving Well Activity Book*. It helps pull out pertinent learning and cements engagement with the text.

Page visual:

Materials needed: Each child needs: Pen, pencil, rubber, sharpener, coloured pens/pencils, activity book. Optional: Scrap paper.

Setting the scene: You may say, *'As we draw closer to the end of the* Leaving Well Activity Book, *we are going to recall what you'd most like to remember'. It's a bit like finishing a sports event. You might have seen a podium where the best competitors stand at the end. You might have even stood on one of these yourself. This page invites you to place on your podium the most important things you want to remember from this activity book'.*

Completing the activity:

1) Feel free to offer a summary of the things you have covered from the *Leaving Well Activity Book*.

Facilitator's top tip: You may like to ask the children to close their eyes as you recount the different things covered to help them recall what's important.

2) Ask the child/ren to come up with three things that they'd like to remember and rank them 1–3, with 1 being the most important. Ask them to write these three things on their podium in the respective boxes. You may like to offer scrap paper for them to make their rough list first.
3) Find a way for sharing of podiums.

Closure: You may say, '*Everyone's podium is different, just like every person and their journey is different. Thank you for thinking so carefully about yours and what you'd like to remember from your* Leaving Well Activity Book'.

*****

Leaving Well Activity Book

Page title: Coping Cube.

Page no: 31

Page rationale: The coping cube is a playful integration activity that encourages the child/ren to identify six coping strategies. Recognising these increases the chances of engaging in a self-regulatory activity at times of need.

Page visual:

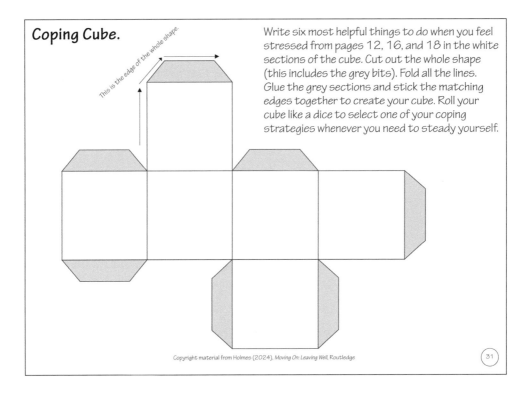

Coping Cube.

This is the edge of the whole shape.

Write six most helpful things to do when you feel stressed from pages 12, 16, and 18 in the white sections of the cube. Cut out the whole shape (this includes the grey bits). Fold all the lines. Glue the grey sections and stick the matching edges together to create your cube. Roll your cube like a dice to select one of your coping strategies whenever you need to steady yourself.

31

Materials needed: Each child needs: Pen, pencil, rubber, sharpener, coloured pens/pencils, activity book, scissors, and glue. Optional: Scrap paper as needed.

Setting the scene: You may say, *'You will create your own coping cube today. When it's finished, the cube will be a die you can roll for a bit of fun and for times when you feel stressed. When you roll your die, the side facing upwards will reveal a coping strategy for you to try'.*

Facilitator's top tip: It may help to have a completed cube to show the child/ren. This will help them visualise what the end result will look like.

Facilitator's top tip: You may like to use a copy of page 31 to demonstrate the folding and cutting procedures with a blank cube. Feel free to copy the page visual in the *Leaving Well Activity Book* for this purpose.

Completing the activity:

1) Encourage the child/ren to read their completed pages 12, 16 and 18. Ask them to make a list of six of the of the most helpful strategies to try when they need to steady themselves. They can make this list on page 31, or a separate piece of paper. If you are supporting one child, you may record their strategies for them in some way.

2) Once they have their six coping strategies, ask them to write one in each of the six white boxes of the coping cube.

3) Next, get them to cut out the cube, including the grey edges, indicated by the arrows on the page.

4) Ask the students to fold along all the lines of the cube. Next, ask them to place glue on the grey parts. Fold into a cuboid, pressing the grey, glued parts underneath the white parts to make a die.

5) Let the child/ren know their cube is ready. In a group setting, you might ask the children to show you their dice by holding them in the air.

Facilitator's top tip: Offer as much help as needed in the construction phase of the coping cube creation. For some, the cutting out and/or the creating the cube itself might be challenging.

Facilitator's top tip: Some children may prefer to draw pictures rather than write on their cube; offer this as an option if you think it helpful.

Closure: You may say, '*So, now you have your very own coping cube. Roll it to help you choose a coping strategy when you need one. I look forward to hearing about ways it helped you*'.

Extension activity: You may like to invite the child/ren to try out their coping cube whilst they are with you. Encourage them to roll their dice and engage in what is written on the section of the die facing upwards.

In a group setting, you may like to pair up the children to talk to each other about their coping cube.

*****

Leaving Well Activity Book

Page title: Awards Ceremony.

Page no: 33

Page rationale: This closure and integration activity invites the child/ren to reflect on their experience of engaging with the *Leaving Well Activity Book*. It helps pull out pertinent learning, cement experience, and appreciate efforts.

Page visual:

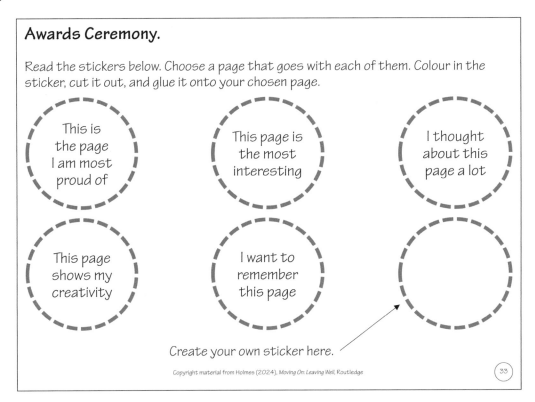

Materials needed: Each child needs: Pen, pencil, rubber, sharpener, coloured pens/pencils, activity book, scissors, and glue.

Setting the scene: You may say. *'You have worked hard to complete the pages of this book. Now, it's time to give some self-appreciation, by giving yourself six awards'.*

Completing the activity:

1) Invite the children to read through the awards on the page silently to themselves or you may choose to read them aloud.

2) Ask the children to colour in each of the stickers.

3) Invite them to write an additional award they would like to give themselves in the blank circle if they wish.

4) Next, ask the child/ren to cut out the stickers and place them on the desk in front of them.

5) Invite them to choose a sticker, match it to their chosen page, and stick it in. Repeat with the remaining five stickers.

6) Ask them to show you, or a partner which sticker they placed on which page and say as little or as much as they would like about that.

Facilitator's top tip: Assist the child/ren, as necessary, with cutting out the stickers.

Closure: You may say, *'Notice how it feels to acknowledge your hard work It's been great to see you do this and hear which pages you appreciate most'*.

*****

Leaving Well Activity Book

Page title: My well-wishes.

Page no: 35

Page rationale: This page encourages the child/ren to collect well-wishes from people that are important to them. These provide a tangible sense of support and kindness which 'the leaver' carries from their current place to the next.

Page visual:

Materials needed: Each child needs: Pen, pencil, rubber, sharpener, coloured pens/pencils, activity book.

Setting the scene: You may say, *'This last page is just for you. It is a way to collect kind and encouraging messages for your journey ahead from different people and will provide a fond reminder of your time here'.*

Completing the activity:

1) You may say, *'Your task is to find people you'd like to receive well-wishes from and ask them to write on this page'*.

2) If you are supporting one child, you may like to write them a message. In a group setting, you may like to ask the children to exchange well-wishes with each other.

Closure: Congratulate the child/ren on their completion of the pages of their *Leaving Well Activity Book*. Let them know you hope their learnings will help them with the next stage of their adventure.

A big well done to you too for supporting the child/ren's journey through the *Leaving Well Activity Book*.

*****

Arriving Well Activity Book

Page title: Welcome.

Page no: 1

Page rationale: This page welcomes the reader, stating the book's purpose and what to expect from the *Arriving Well Activity Book*. The child begins to take ownership of their process by writing their name and where they are moving from and to.

Page visual:

> Welcome!
>
> You've been given this activity book because you have moved to a new country.
>
> It's a book that helps you learn about arriving well. Each page has a different activity. You'll get creative by drawing, colouring, writing, and making things. It will help you make a great start and settle in your new place.
>
> This book belongs to _____
>
> I have moved from _____ to
>
> _____

Materials needed: Each child needs: Pen, pencil, rubber, sharpener, coloured pens/pencils, activity book. Optional: World map/country floor labels.

Setting the scene: You may say, *'Welcome. You've been given this book to help you arrive and settle well. We are going to have some fun completing the pages together, I'm here to help and answer any questions. If you are ready to get creative, let's begin...'.*

Completing the activity:

1) Read the two paragraphs on the page out loud or ask the child/ren to read it themselves.
2) Ask the child/ren to write their name and where they are moving from and to on the lines provided.

3) If you are a parent supporting your child, you may like to proceed to page 2 now. You may say, *'Let's turn over to let's turn to the next page and get our crayons/coloured pencils/felt tip pens at the ready'*.

4) As teachers/therapists, if you are supporting one child, you may ask them where they have moved from and when they arrived in the current country. In a group setting, there are various options; you may invite the children to share the country they have moved from out loud or in pairs. If the children are shared in pairs, you might like to include an activity where the children introduce their partner, telling the group their partner's name and the country they moved from. Alternatively, you might get the students to imagine there is a world map on the floor. Indicate where Australia and New Zealand are with the USA and Canada on the other side (you might need a visual of a world map or labels on the floor). Ask them to roughly position themselves in the country they have come from. Ask the children to tell the group the country they last lived in from the position they are standing in.

Facilitator's top tip: Highlight to the child/children that everyone's life story is different and special. You may say, *'That's what makes moving so interesting; we get to meet so many people with different experiences'*.

Closure: You may say, *'Thank you for sharing I am really looking forward to hearing more as we move through the* Arriving Well Activity Book. *Let's turn over to turn to the next page and get our crayons/coloured pencils/felt tip pens at the ready'*.

Extension activity: You may like to ask the child/ren to count on their fingers how many countries they have lived in, including their current one. Ask them to hold their hand up to show how many fingers they have selected. Find a way for the child/ren to list the countries they have lived in. You may like to show your own number of countries you have lived in by showing the appropriate number of fingers too.

In a larger group, ask the students to raise their hand if they have lived in one country or more (all hands should be raised). Ask students to keep their hand up if they have lived in two countries or more and to lower their hand if they have lived in one country only; then, keep their hand up if they have lived in three countries or more and to lower their hand if they have lived in two countries. Keep moving up number of countries in this way until only one child's hand is raised (or there is a tie). Invite group member/s with the greatest number to share the countries they have lived in.

You could also try this activity with students standing and sitting down when appropriate instead of raising and lowering hands.

*****

Arriving Well Activity Book

Page title: Your life story.

Page no: 2 & 3

Page rationale: These pages invite the child/ren to create a timeline of significant events in their life so far. Doing so can be empowering and affirming. These pages help with understanding that transitions and change are part of life.

Page visual:

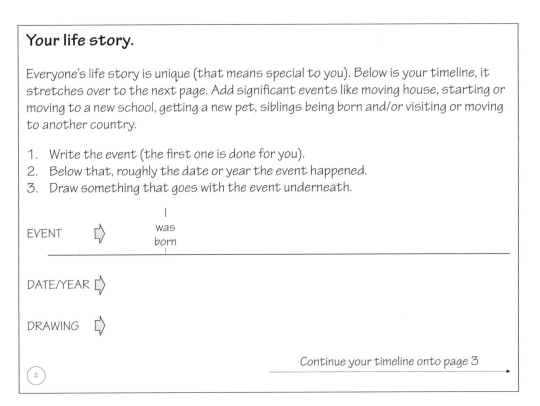

```
┌─────────────────────────────────────────────────────────────────────┐
│ Change happens.                                                       │
│                                                                       │
│ Change is a normal part of life; we've all been through transitions   │
│ (which means moving from one thing to another). Put a star by the     │
│ events that are transitions on your timeline. The last one is done    │
│ for you.                                                              │
│                                                                       │
│                                                              *I        │
│                                                            moved       │
│                                                              to        │
│                                                                       │
│                                                                       │
│ ─────────────────────────────────────────────────     ┌ ─ ─ ─ ┐     │
│                                                                       │
│                                                                       │
│                                                                       │
│ ──────────────────────────────────────────►                    (3)   │
└─────────────────────────────────────────────────────────────────────┘
```

Materials needed: Each child needs: Pen, pencil, rubber, sharpener, coloured pens/pencils, activity book.

Setting the scene: You may say, *'Pages 2 & 3 give you the opportunity to think about your life story. You'll create a timeline to show significant events in your life so far. Each person's timeline will be different and special'.*

Completing the activity:

1) You may say, *'Begin by opening your books so you can see both pages 2 & 3 in front of you. You'll notice there is a line that goes across both pages. With a pencil, join up these two lines as best you can'.* Allow child/ren time to do this. *'The lines you joined make your timeline. A timeline is a way of showing events in the order they happened through your life so far'.*

2) Still using pencils (as things can be rubbed out if they get the order wrong) invite the chid/ren to finish the 'I was born' entry on their timeline by adding the date below the writing and then drawing a picture underneath the date to represent the event.

3) Next, ask the children to look at the other end of their timeline on page 3; ask them to write the country they are in now on the line underneath 'I moved to _____', add the date and draw something that goes with that.

4) You may say, '*After you've done that, think of other significant (which means important) events that have happened in between the two entries you've made, things like moving house, changing schools, getting a new pet, siblings being born, visiting or moving to another country*'.

5) Give the child/ren time to make several entries on their timeline.

Facilitator's top tip: You may invite the child/ren to brainstorm major events in their life using the blank 'brain dump' page at the back of the activity book (page 35).

6) Next, read them the text at the top of page 3. Invite them to add stars by the events that are transitions.

7) Find the most approriate way for sharing of what they have entered on their timeline with you/a partner/the group.

Facilitator's top tip: If you are in a school/therapeutic setting, this may be an activity the child/ren continue at home. You may encourage them to show their parents/guardians these pages to see if they can help add additional events.

Facilitator's top tip: If you have some star stickers, you may like to offer these to the child/ren to add to their timeline instead of drawing them.

Closure: You may say, '*Now you've created you own timeline and added stars; you probably notice most of the things on your timeline are transitions. Remember change is a normal part of life. As humans we are programmed to cope with change; it can be tough, especially when we expierience many, but each time you go through a transition, you practise coping with change*'.

Extension activity: You may like to encourage the child/ren to stick in small photos and/or images to their timeline.

*****

Arriving Well Activity Book

Page title: Where are you now?

Page no: 4

Page rationale: This page offers an opportunity to reflect. The child/ren are invited to draw what best represents their new country inside a circle. A circle is a reoccurring theme in healing across many cultures. The experience of creating a circular, visual representation of the new place encourages curiosity and connection. No two circles will be the same.

Page visual:

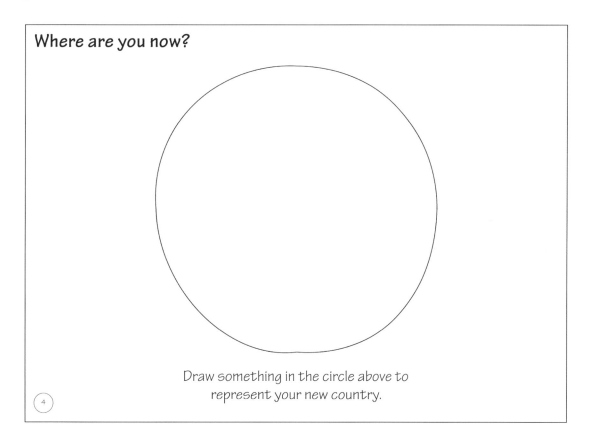

Where are you now?

Draw something in the circle above to represent your new country.

4

Materials needed: Each child needs: Pen, pencil, rubber, sharpener, coloured pens/pencils, activity book.

Setting the scene: You may say, *'This page invites you to get creative by thinking about what best represents your new country in a picture'.*

Completing the activity:

1) Before they begin, ask them, *'When you think of the country you live in now what do you think of? What seems to best represent _____?'* (Add the name of the country here). You can do this verbally or use a white board/digital medium to record responses.

Facilitator's top tip: You may like to give an example of what you would draw in the circle if you were the artist.

2) You may say, *'It doesn't need to be a perfect artwork. You can draw specific things or be more abstract using colours, shapes lines, and/or squiggles'.*

Facilitator's top tip: Have a variety of art material ready. The child/ren may like to print out pictures to add; you could have some ready for them to use too.

Facilitator's top tip: Some children may take longer than others to do this task. If you feel you'd like to move on before the child/ren have finished do so, give an option to finish their piece at another time. This may even be a page you ask the child/ren to complete in their own time. As teachers/therapists, if you'd rather keep the book with you, give them a blank circle to take with them which can be stuck in later.

Closure: You may say, *'Thank you for using your artistic skills. I hope you are pleased with your creation'.*

Extension activity: You might like to ask the artist/s to give their piece a title. If you are working with one child, you might like to set up a role play; invite the child to pretend their artwork is in an exhibition. Tell them you are a visitor to the exhibition and challenge them, as the artist, to tell you the title and as much as they can about their piece.

In a group setting, you may invite group members to introduce (using the art exhibition example above, if you wish) their artwork one by one, sharing the title and something brief about their creation.

Perhaps creating an interactive gallery of sorts appeals; you may like to get the children moving around the room, sharing their piece with another child, then moving to another when they are ready, or on your signal.

Another suggestion is to create a gallery by laying out the artworks for the group to view.

*****

Arriving Well Activity Book

Page title: Feelings wheel.

Page no: 5

Page rationale: This page encourages child/ren to acknowledge feelings. Being able to name and share feelings has a regulatory effect. Dan Siegel, Professor of Psychiatry at UCLA School of Medicine, coined the concept of 'name it to tame it'. Naming feelings reduces their intensity, which helps to gain a greater sense of control. Facilitation of this page seeks to help children understand it's normal to experience a range of feelings at times of transition and all are okay.

Page visual:

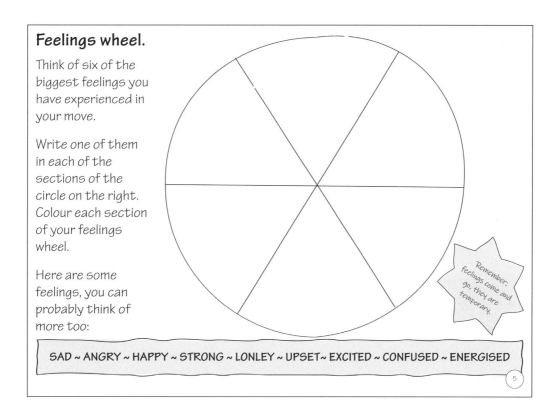

Materials needed: Each child needs: Pen, pencil, rubber, sharpener, coloured pens/pencils, activity book.

Setting the scene: You may say, *'This page is about feelings. It's normal to experience lots of big feelings when moving from one place to another. Naming feelings helps to manage them better; everyone feels different; there's no right or wrong way to feel'.*

Completing the activity:

1) You may say, *'You will see your feelings wheel on your page. When this page is complete, each section of the wheel will contain a feeling. Can you name one big feeling you have noticed during this time of change?'* Direct the child/ren to the bottom of the page as needed.

2) Invite the child/ren to write a feeling in one of the sections of their feelings wheel. Ask the children to share the feeling they have chosen. If you are in a group setting, invite them to share with the group. If time allows, you may ask, *'When did you notice the feeling most?'* You may share, *'Thanks for telling me your big feeling. It might have taken a lot of courage. When you name feelings, you feel more in control. A good way to remember this is, "Name it to tame it!" To tame something means you can manage it better. The interesting thing about feelings is they are temporary, which means they come and go, as it says in the grey star on your page'.*

3) Next, ask the child/ren to colour in the section of the feelings wheel they wrote their feeling in with a colour that best matches that feeling. Let them know that it doesn't need to be a solid colour, they can create a pattern if they wish.

4) Continue for the next five feelings, you may choose to use the same format or let the child/ren write their feeling and colour the corresponding section at their own pace.

5) At the end of the activity, ask the child/ren if anything stood out to them as they created their feelings wheel.

Facilitator's top tip: If some children finish before others, invite them to decorate their page and/or add any other feelings they can think of to the list at the bottom.

Closure: You may say, *'All feelings wheels are different because we are all unique and special. Next time you notice one of these big feelings arrive, see if you can name it (remember that tames it). Becoming curious and interested in your feelings helps to understand yourself better and be able to be more in control of these big feelings when need be'.*

*****

Arriving Well Activity Book

Page title: Listen to your body and speak kindly to yourself.

Page no: 6

Page rationale: This page develops interoception. Interoception is the ability to sense signals from the body. When interoception is honed, our ability to answer the question 'how do I feel?' at any given moment is increased. Kelly Mahler, a world-renowned occupational therapist, says that interoception has a huge influence on many areas of our lives like self-regulation, mental health, and social connection. This page helps the child get familiar with their 'Stress Signature' and encourages the child/ren to pay attention to what they say to themselves. It is hoped their 'Arriving Well Message' becomes an important part of their coping in coming weeks.

Page visual:

Materials needed: Each child needs: Pen, pencil, rubber, sharpener, coloured pens/pencils, activity book.

Setting the scene: You may say, *'We are going to think about the six big feelings from the last page and where you feel these in your body. On this page you'll also think of a helpful thing to say to yourself when these big feelings arrive; this will help you feel more in control.*

Completing the activity:

1) Invite the child/ren to start with one of their big feelings from their feelings wheel on the last page. Ask them to take a moment to think about where they notice this feeling in their body, highlighting that everyone's experience is different. You may like to ask, *'Where does that feeling show up in your body?'*, *'Does it have a colour?'*, *'Does it have a shape?'*, *'Is there a symbol, like a boat, star, tree, or animal that fits with this feeling?'*, *'If you were to draw it, would it have straight lines, curvy lines, dotted lines, or maybe some squiggles?'* If you are supporting one child, you can explore this 1-1; in a group setting, you may like to invite wider sharing.

Facilitator's top tip: If the child/ren are strugglling to tune into their somatic experience, you may ask, *'Last time you were feeling stressed or overwhelmed, what do you remember happened inside your body? Perhaps a fast heartbeat, breathing quicker, a churned up feeling in your tummy, fidgety arms/legs, a clenched jaw or fist, maybe even going red or sweating. Do any of these sounds familiar?* Ask which of these responses are true for them. They may be able to add other things that happened in their body to the list. Invite them to return to page 5. Ask them if they can link any of the bodily responses to a feeling listed on their wheel.

2) Next, invite the child/ren to add colours, shapes, symbols, lines, and/or squiggles to their body outline on page 6 to represent where they feel the feeling in their body.
3) Repeat for the remaining five feelings. The child/ren can work at their own pace or you may choose to repeat 1), 2), and 3) for each of the feelings.
4) Invite the child/ren to read the text in the grey box, or you may choose to read this aloud.
5) Encourage them to write their 'Arriving Well Message'. Make the connection with noticing big feelings arriving in their body and recalling their message to steady themselves.

Facilitator's top tip: If the child/ren are strugglling to think of a message, ask them what a good friend might say to help them at a time of overwhelm. If an adult they are close to works better for them, go with that.

Closure: You may say, *'Thank you for thinking so carefully about where you notice your feelings in your body and your 'Arriving Well Message'. After our time together, you might like to continue this curiosity and notice where different feelings turn up in your body. You might like to pause, notice, and remember your message'.*

Extension activity: You might like to invite the child/ren to write their 'Arriving Well Message' on a post-it note and put it up somewhere helpful for them. Another suggestion may be to write it on their bathroom or bedroom mirror with a glass marker, so that they see their message daily.

*****

Arriving Well Activity Book

Page title: Keep your breath in mind.

Page no: 7

Page rationale: Mountain Breathing is a way to regulate breathing. Regulated breathing helps the mind and body to settle by triggering the bodies' physiological relaxation response. Mountain Breathing is a handy strategy to include in the child/ren's self-regulation toolbox.

Page visual:

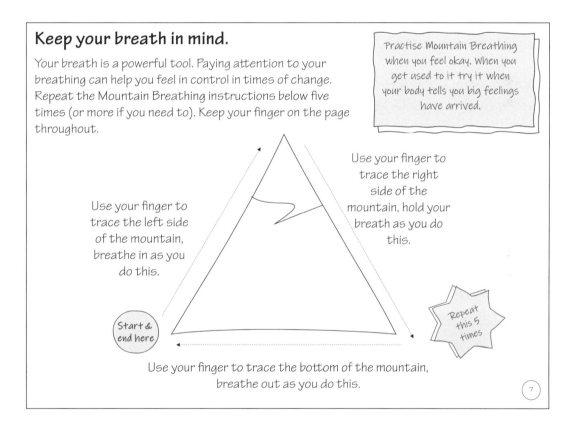

Materials needed: Each child needs: Pen, pencil, rubber, sharpener, coloured pens/pencils, activity book.

Setting the scene: You may say, *'At times of change, paying attention to your breath can help to feel more in control. This page teaches you a breathing tool (tool means something that's helpful) to steady yourself when big feelings arrive or when you want to feel more relaxed'.*

Completing the activity:

1) Before the child/ren begin, you might ask them to choose one word to describe how their mind and body feels – give an example of your own, *e.g. 'My mind feels busy; my body feels heavy'.* There is no right or wrong. Challenge the child/ren to stick to one word.
2) You might like to ask the child/ren if they have climbed a mountain before? Let them know the breathing tool they are going to learn is called Mountain Breathing.
3) Ask the child/ren to get themselves comfortable. They might need to adjust their position a little.
4) Guide them through the instructions for Mountain Breathing on their page.
5) After going through five rounds, repeat 1) above. You might like to reflect on their answers briefly by highlighting (if appropriate) that *'Mountain Breathing has helped to relax your body and mind'*.

Facilitator's top tip: Consider showing the child/ren they can trace a traingle shape in the air or on their hand to practise Mountian Breathing.

Facilitator's top tip: You may choose to begin your next session with Mountain Breathing together, creating a link between one session and the next.

Closure: Remind the child/ren to practise Mountain Breathing when they feel okay, to be able to use it when they are feeling overwhelmed. You might like to give them a challenge to practise it every day until you meet again.

Extension activity: To help the child/ren stay connected to Mountain Breathing, you might encourage them to teach this skill to someone else and report back next time you meet.

You may like to challenge the child/ren to come up with their own breathing shape. Mountain Breathing uses a triangle; can they think of any other shapes they could trace or visualise to relegate their breathing?

*****

Arriving Well Activity Book

Page title: Ground yourself.

Page no: 8

Page rationale: 54321 is a practice that can be called upon to ground oneself. It's a mindful activity that uses the senses to anchor in the present. By choosing to focus on the present moment, we escort the mind away from dysregulating thoughts that are past- or future-orientated.

Page visual:

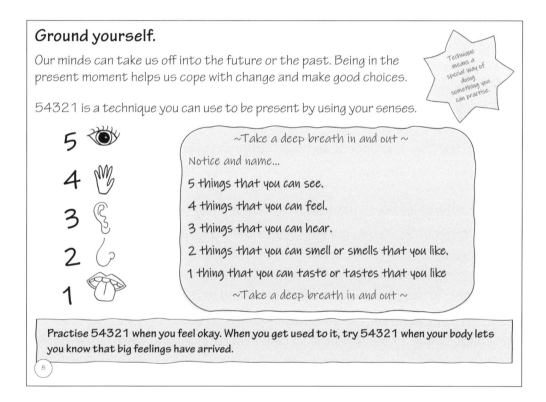

Materials needed: Each child needs: activity book.

Setting the scene: You may say, *'We are going to learn a technique (technique means a special way of doing something that you can practise) called 54321. It uses your five senses. It's a way to ground yourself, which is another way of saying you feel steady and solid. 54321 helps to bring your mind back to what's happening now, rather than your mind wandering off into the future or past. Being in the present moment helps you think more clearly and make good decisions'.*

Facilitator's top tip: The child/ren may ask you, 'What is the present moment?' You may say, *'The present moment is right now, not in the past or the future. For example, can you pay attention what you can hear now?* Get them to do this briefly. You may say, *'When you do this, you are placing your attention on sounds happening in this present moment'.*

Completing the activity:

1) Before the child/ren begin, you might ask them to choose one word to describe how their mind and body feels – give an example of your own, *e.g. 'My mind feels busy; my body feels heavy'.* There is no right or wrong. Challenge the child/ren to stick to one word.

2) Ask the child/ren to get themselves comfortable. They might need to adjust their position a little. Let them know to 'ground' themselves; it helps to put both feet flat on the floor.

3) Guide them through the instructions for 54321 on the page. If they are in a group setting, ask them to silently name things they can see, feel, hear, smell, and taste. If you are supporting one child, you may like to get them to practice 54321 out loud.

4) After completing the exercise, repeat 1) above. You might like to reflect on their answers briefly by highlighting (if appropriate) that *'54321 has helped to relax your body and mind'.*

Facilitator's top tip: You may choose to begin your next session with 54321, creating a link between one session and the next.

Closure: Remind the child/ren to practise 54321 when they feel okay, to be able to use it when feeling overwhelmed. You might like to give them a challenge to practise it every day until you meet again.

Extension activity: To help the child/ren stay connected to 54321, you might encourage them to teach it to someone else and to report back next time you meet. You may copy and share the '54321' image below for the child/ren to take away and remind them of the exercise.

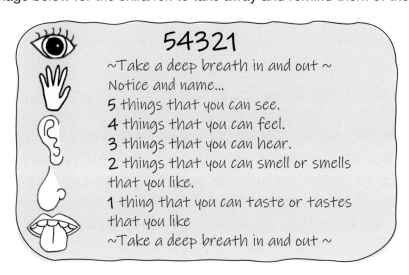

*****

Arriving Well Activity Book

Page title: Moving on graph.

Page no: 9

Page rationale: The moving on graph on this page describes a typical experience of relocating to a new country. The graph is based on the U-Curve Adjustment Theory coined by Norwegian sociologist Sverre Lysgaard in 1955. Since then, it's been used and adapted widely to help understand cultural adaptation. The child/ren locate themselves on the graph and are given the opportunity to acknowledge their emotional journey so far. This page looks to foster acceptance for whatever feelings are noticed and normalise mixed emotions. Wellbeing is defined, a theme that runs through the book.

Page visual:

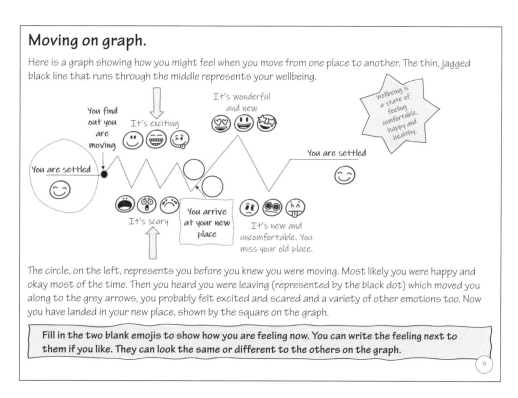

Materials needed: Each child needs: Pen, pencil, rubber, sharpener, coloured pens/pencils, activity book.

Setting the scene: You may say, '*On this page is a graph showing how you might feel when you move from one place to another. Everyone's experience is different but there are things many people notice when moving to a new country that are the same. Let's have a look at this graph*'.

Completing the activity:

1) You may say, '*The first thing to notice is the thin, jagged line that runs through the middle of the graph. That represents your wellbeing. Wellbeing can be described as feeling comfortable, happy, and healthy*'.

2) Get the child/ren to trace the line from left to right with their finger. Ask them, what they notice about the line as they do this. (Draw out that the line moves up and down). Let them know that wellbeing is like this, it's 'up and down'; some days you feel better than others.

3) Ask them to place their finger on the circle and what it says inside. When they reply, 'You are settled', let them know this circle represents them before they knew they were moving. (If they ask what settled means, say, '*It's feeling comfortable with where you are*'.)

4) Say, '*Then you find out that you are moving*' – ask them to move their finger along to the small black circle.

5) Ask them to keep tracing until they get to the grey arrows. Ask, '*What happens to the line?*' (They will notice it goes up and down quickly/sharply). Say, '*This is where you most likely experienced a roller coaster of emotions. Probably feeling sad one minute and excited the next, and lots of other feelings too*'.

6) You may say, '*Then it was time to arrive here*'. Ask the child/ren to trace their finger along to the square that says, 'You arrive at your new place'.

7) You may say, '*Think about what you are feeling now, or were feeling when you first arrived and create two emojis to represent those feelings in the two blank circles on your page*'.

8) The child/ren can choose to write the feeling next to the emojis they have drawn, if they like.

9) Find a way for the child/ren to share their emojis.

Facilitator's top tip: Highlight whatever emotions they are feeling are okay, remind the child/ren that everyone's journey is unique and different.

Closure: You may say, '*Noticing and naming feelings can help be more in control. It's sometimes tough to talk about how you are feeling but it does help*'.

*****

Arriving Well Activity Book

Page title: Pros (things that are good) and cons (things that are not so good).

Page no: 10

Page rationale: Arriving well is aided by having a balanced view of what's working and what's not working so well. Awareness of each of these things lets us celebrate 'the good' and make plans to address the challenges.

Page visual:

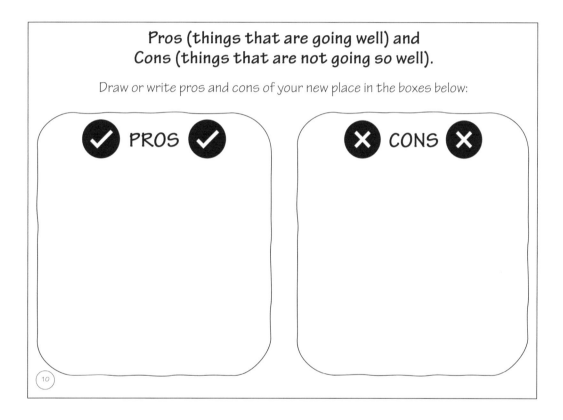

Materials needed: Each child needs: Pen, pencil, rubber, sharpener, coloured pens/pencils, activity book.

Setting the scene: You may say, *'It's normal that some things will be going well, and some things are tricky when you arrive in a new place. This page helps you identify things that are working (these are the pros) and things that are not working so well (these are the cons)'.*

Completing the activity:

1) You may say, *'You'll see two boxes on the page. Let's start with the right-hand side, the cons; these are the things not working so well, things you are finding challenging about your new place. Some examples might be the weather, where you are living, friends, school subjects, the food here'.*

Facilitator's top tip: Starting with the cons allows you to conclude your facilitation on a positive note.

2) You may say, *'Think about what the cons are and draw or write them inside the box on the right'.*
3) When they have done this, you may say, *'Is there anything that you could do more of or less of to make the cons go a little better for you? Write or draw what this might be next to the cons you have listed'.*
4) Find a way for the child/ren to share. If time is limited, they can share one of their cons and their idea for making it a little better.

Facilitator's top tip: Remind the children that settling in takes a while and some of their cons will get better over time.

5) Next, invite the child/ren to draw or write their pros in the left-hand box.
6) When they have done this, you may say, *'Is there anything you can keep doing to increase the chances of the pros continuing? Write or draw what this might be next to the pros you have listed'.*
7) Find a way for the child/ren to share. If time is limited, they can share one of their pros and their suggestion for increasing the chances of it continuing well.

Closure: You may say, *'Thanks for thinking about things that are going well and things you would like to be going better. Please remember that it takes time to arrive and settle, if I asked you to fill this page in a few weeks from now, it would look quite different. If any of these things on this page becomes too difficult for you to handle, be sure to tell an understanding adult about it'.*

Extension activity: If time permits, you may ask the child/ren who that understanding adult might be. You may even like to 'fast forward' to page 28 of the *Arriving Well Activity Book*, which invites the child/ren to name three people they can ask for help.

*****

Arriving Well Activity Book

Page title: Mindful colouring.

Page no: 11

Page rationale: Many children (and adults!) find mindful colouring a way to anchor themselves in the present moment. Used as a regulation strategy, mindful colouring is a way to remind our body and mind how to relax. The more often we engage in relaxing activities, the better we get at creating calm.

Page visual:

Materials needed: Each child needs: Coloured pens/pencils activity book. Optional: Soothing music, timer.

Setting the scene: You may say, *'When you are mindful, you choose where to place your attention. Mindful colouring helps take care of your mind as you are choosing to place your attention on something creative. When you do this, your mind rests in the present, rather than worrying about what's going to happen or has happened. Mindful colouring helps your body to relax too'.*

Facilitator's top tip: The child/ren may ask you, 'What is the present moment?' You may say, *'The present moment is right now, not in the past or the future. For example, can you pay attention what you see now?* Get them to do this briefly. You may say, *'When you do this, you are placing your attention on your visual field (what you can see), tuning into what's happening in this present moment'.*

Completing the activity:

1) Before the child/ren begin, ask them to choose one word to describe how their mind and body feels – give an example of your own, *e.g. 'My mind feels busy; my body feels heavy'.* There is no right or wrong. Challenge the child/ren to stick to one word.

2) Once the child/ren have begun colouring, you may say, *'As you colour, notice your feet flat on the floor, give your feet a little wiggle if you like. As you keep colouring, notice your breathing, be aware you are breathing in and out. You might like to make the in-breath and the out-breath slightly longer'.*

3) At the end of your mindful colouring time, repeat 1) above. You might like to reflect on their answers by highlighting (if appropriate), *'Isn't it curious how mindful colouring has made a difference to your body and mind?'*

Facilitator's top tip: Have a variety of different pens and pencils accessible, so that the child/ren stay seated whilst colouring.

Facilitator's top tip: You might like to show the child/ren an example of a completed page so they can see how their page may look.

Facilitator's top tip: Children will progress with this page at different rates; you might like to set a timer.

Facilitator's top tip: Playing relaxing music whilst the child/ren mindfully colour helps create a calm atmosphere.

Closure: You may say, *'Every time you practice mindful colouring, you are reminding your body and mind how to relax. You might like to try this activity when you notice stress showing up in your body to help steady yourself. Thanks for being creative today'.*

Extension activity: To encourage reflection, you may ask *'What did you discover during that activity?'* They may discuss this with you, or in a group setting, in pairs, or the wider group.

*****

Arriving Well Activity Book

Page title: Move your body to lift your mood.

Page no: 12

Page rationale: Moving your body boosts wellbeing. Exercise releases feel good hormones that lift mood, and breaks down stress hormones. Doing something active helps shift stuck energy and to think more clearly. This page helps children identify ways to move their body and consider how they would like to be active in their new place. Doing something active has the added benefit of increasing the chances of making new connections with other children doing the same thing. Lastly, there is substantial research that speaks of the transformative power of nature on wellbeing; this page explores what might be possible for the child.

Page visual:

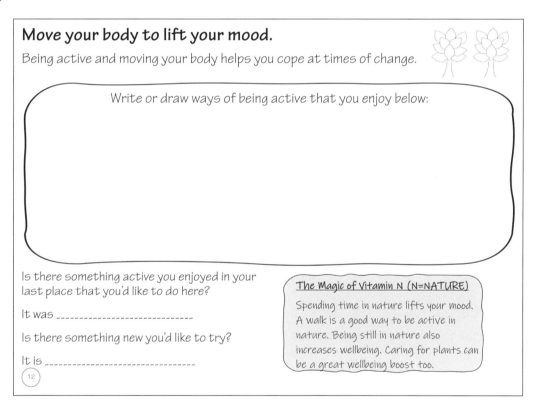

Materials needed: Each child needs: Pen, pencil, rubber, sharpener, coloured pens/pencils, activity book.

Setting the scene: Read the title and the first line of the page out loud. You may say, *'This page will help you think about active things you enjoy, new ways of moving your body, and appreciate that time in nature boosts wellbeing'.*

Completing the activity:

1) You may say, *'So, let's begin with recording one way of being active that you like in the box, you can write or draw it'.*

Facilitator's top tip: You may give examples of things other children have mentioned before; going to the park, playing football, riding a bike or scooter, walking to school or in their neighbourhood, trampolining, watersports, or walking their dog. Make examples as relevent as possible to your setting.

2) Give the students time to record their activity. As they are doing so, you might say, *'People like different things and we are going to learn from each other today.'*
3) Find a way for each child to share their activity. If you are working with one child, they can tell you what it is, act it out, charades style, or give verbal clues without naming the activity. This may also be possible in a group setting.
4) Invite the child/ren to carry on adding different activites they like to do. If you are supporting one child, encourage sharing as they draw or write. In a group setting, move around the group being curious about what activities child/ren have recorded.
5) Next, bring attention to the bottom left of the page and ask the child/ren to fill in the gaps.
6) Find a way for the child/ren to share what they have written. Give some ideas of how they might be able to find out what's on offer or join activities they have mentioned.
7) Next, bring the child/ren's attention to the grey box, bottom right of the page. Read this out loud or invite them to read it silently to themselves.
8) Find a way to explore what the child/ren already do in nature and find out if they would like spend more time in a natural envirmonent. Invite them to add anything pertinant after this discussion.

Facilitator's top tip: You may like to lead the 'Peaceful place in nature visualisation' (shared in the Extension activity below) and explain that even imagining a place in nature can boost wellbeing.

Closure: You may say, *'We've explored a lot on this page. Think about what you would like to remember after we finish. Perhaps there was an activity you'd like to try?'*

Extension activity: If time permits, you may consider leading a short stroll in nature. Alternatively, you may choose to show some photos of natural places nearby that the child/ren can explore in their own time, or you may like to invite the child/ren to plant some seeds to care for over the coming weeks in a pot or garden.

Peaceful place in nature visualisation:

The script below is designed to lead the child/ren whilst they are seated on a chair. Feel free to adjust the script if child/ren are in a different position.

Sit in a comfortable position, place your feet flat on the floor, if possible.
Allow your eyes to close.
Notice your body in contact with the chair.
Be aware of your breath, breathing in and breathing out.
Bring to mind a beautiful, peaceful place somewhere in nature.
It could be a forest, a beach, a place where the weather is cold or hot. It could be a place you've been to, perhaps somewhere you've seen in a photograph or a completely imaginary place.
Let that place become clearer in your mind. (Pause).
Imagine you are in your peaceful place in nature now. I am going to invite you to use your five senses to explore.
Notice what you can see. (Pause).
Notice what you can hear. (Pause).
Notice what you can touch, imagine yourself moving around your space if you need to. (Pause).
Notice what you can smell. (Pause).
Notice any tastes. (Pause).
Take a few deep breaths, notice how safe and soothing your natural place feels.
You might like to spend a little longer connecting with your place in nature, noticing whatever calls for your attention. (Pause).
Know that you can return to your peaceful place in nature anytime you need to.
Say goodbye to your peaceful place, now, letting it go.
Be aware of your breath, breathing in and breathing out.
Notice your body in contact with the chair.
Your feet flat on the floor.
Open your eyes, coming back into this room'.

Facilitator's top tip: After the visualisation, you may ask the children to describe their peaceful place to you/partner or group.

You may invite the children to draw their peaceful place and share as appropriate.

Suggest they have a go at 'visiting' their peaceful place in their mind when they are feeling okay. When they get used to doing this, they might find it helpful to 'return' there in moments of overwhelm.

*****

Arriving Well Activity Book

Page title: It's wonderful and new.

Page no: 13

Page rationale: This page shares the moving on graph again and pays attention to the 'honeymoon' period that most people experience when moving to a new country. It's often described as a feeling of euphoria; everything feels wonderful and new, different, and okay. This page works on the premise that if children understand their emotional experiences, they will stay connected to themselves over this period of change.

Page visual:

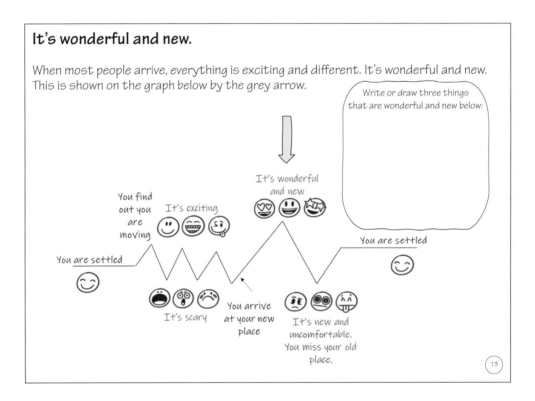

Materials needed: Each child needs: Pen, pencil, rubber, sharpener, coloured pens/pencils, activity book.

Setting the scene: You may say, *'This page returns to the graph we saw on an earlier page. Place your finger on the peak that says, "It's wonderful and new". Often when people arrive in a new country, they experience a time of finding everything wonderful and new'.*

Facilitator's top tip: You might like to preface this page with a short quiz, sharing photos/slides of a few unique things about your country or school that the child/ren may have found wonderful and new. You could include food, attractions to visit, school facilities, something about their new home, language, dance, music, and/or animals as a few examples.

Completing the activity:

1) Ask the child/ren if they have noticed anything wonderful and new here. Perhaps share some examples of your own.
2) When you have been through a few examples, invite them to list three wonderful and new things in the box on the page.
3) Ask the children if they can remember what the thin, black jagged line on the graph represents (Answer-wellbeing: A state of feeling comfortable, happy, and healthy). Ask what they notice happens to this line when someone finds everything wonderful and new (Answer-wellbeing increases).

Facilitator's top tip: This page and the next fit together well. If possible, guide pages 13 & 14 in one session.

Closure: You may say, *'So, you've thought about things feeling wonderful and new, you'll notice that the thin, black, jagged line dips down as we follow the graph along. The next page looks at what might happen next as you settle in, you may find you start to miss where you came from. This is a normal part of transition and the things we are going to talk about will help you move along the graph to the right of the page where it says, "you are settled"'.*

*****

Arriving Well Activity Book

Page title: Missing where you came from.

Page no: 14

Page rationale: This page returns to the moving on graph and pays attention to the likely period of 'culture shock' that someone moving to a new country may experience. This is characterised by feeling that things are different and not okay; wellbeing takes a dip, and the 'arriver' misses their old place. This page normalises 'the dip' in mood that may impact wellbeing after arriving. Raising children's awareness of this potential emotional dip increases the chances of them being equipped to move through this phase with more ease. The child/ren are asked to think about three things they will be doing when they are settled, utilising the presupposition that they WILL settle, fostering a sense of hope.

Page visual:

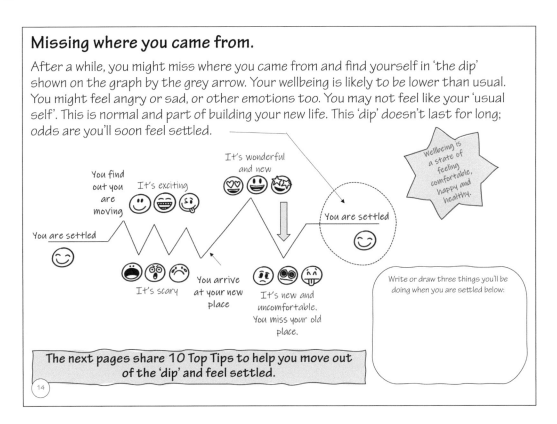

Materials needed: Each child needs: Pen, pencil, rubber, sharpener, coloured pens/pencils, activity book.

Setting the scene: You may say, *'This page follows on from the last. It will help you understand how you may feel after everything feels wonderful and new. It's normal, after a while, that things start to feel new and uncomfortable, and you miss your old place. Don't worry, this feeling won't last forever. Let's find out more…'.*

Completing the activity:

1) You may say, *'This page is called "Missing where you came from". It's normal to miss things about your last place as you settle'.*

2) You may like to ask the child/ren if there are things they miss about their old place and if so, what they are. Find a way for sharing.

3) Read the paragraph on the page out loud to the child/ren. When you mention the grey arrow, ask them to place their finger on it. When you read 'odds are you'll soon feel settled', ask them to move their finger from the arrow to the thin, black line and below and trace with their finger to the circle that says, 'You are settled'.

4) Invite them to look at the box on the bottom left of the page. You may say, *'Eventually you'll feel more settled here. Can you think of three things you will be doing when you are settled? What would indicate you are more comfortable? Write or draw these three things in the box on your page'.*

5) Find a way for the child/ren to share their three things.

Closure: You may say, *'Human beings are designed for survival; you are programmed to face and cope with change. The next few pages of the activity book shares 10 top tips to help increase your chances of arriving well. You'll learn about things to help you move out of 'the dip and feel settled'.*

Extension activity: You may invite the child/ren to notice when the three things they wrote in their box happen, even just a little bit…. ask them to notice where they are, what they are doing, and who they are with. If you choose to do this, you may like to begin your next session checking in on what they discovered.

*****

Arriving Well Activity Book

Page title: Top tip # 1: Be brave.

Page no: 15

Page rationale: This page is the first of 10 top tips for settling well and moving out of 'the dip'. This expressive drawing activity uses creativity to help the child/ren connect with being brave. This page links a few of the concepts already covered; breathing strategies, recognising somatic signs, self-talk, and the 'Arriving Well Message' from page 6.

Page visual:

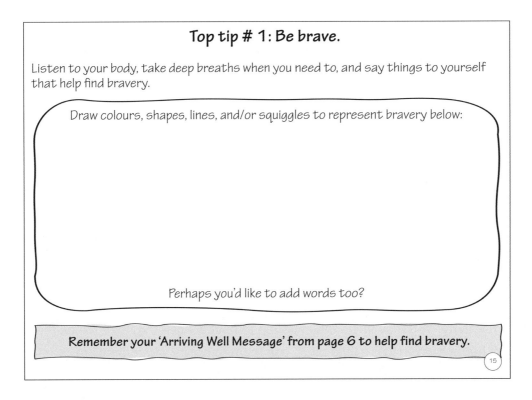

Materials needed: Each child needs: Pen, pencil, rubber, sharpener, coloured pens/pencils, activity book.

Setting the scene: You may say, *'Top tip number one is, "Be brave". Being brave means finding the courage to do something uncomfortable or difficult, like the first day of a new school, joining a new activity, or sitting with a new group of friends. When you notice your body telling you anxious feelings have arrived, it's often a sign you are about to do something brave. It takes bravery to move to a new country and settle in. Let's remember some of the things we've learnt so far that will help with this...'.*

Completing the activity:

1) You may say, *'Chances are, you added worry and/or anxiety to your feelings wheel on page 5'.*

2) Invite the child/ren to turn to page 6 to remind themselves how they notice worry or anxiety in their body. If they didn't include this feeling, you may ask, *'When you feel worried or anxious what do you notice happening in your body?*

3) After the child/ren have shared their somatic signs of worry or anxiety, you may say, *'These signs are your signals that bravery is needed'.*

4) You may say, *'Taking some deep breaths can help you feel braver. Can you remember 'Mountain Breathing?'*

5) Lead the child/ren through the instructions for 'Mountain Breathing' on page 7.

Facilitator's top tip: You may choose to lead your own breathing technique if you wish.

6) After this, ask the child/ren to read their 'Arriving Well Message' on page 6 to themselves.

7) Next, ask the child/ren to draw colours, shapes, lines, and/or squiggles to represent bravery in the box on page 15. You might like to try the 'Exploring bravery visualisation,' outlined in the Extension activity below before the child/ren fill in the box on their page.

8) Invite the child/ren to add words that fit with what they have drawn in their box if they wish.

Closure: You may say, *'Being brave is an important part of arriving well. Listen to your body, notice when worry or anxiety arrives as it's a sure sign you need to awaken bravery. You can do this by regulating your breath and saying encouraging things to yourself. Notice times when you use your courage; the more often you practise it, the better you get at awakening it in times of need'.*

Extension activity: To deepen connection with bravery you might try the 'Exploring bravery visualisation' below:

Exploring bravery visualisation:
Some children will silently notice answers during this activity. Some may answer you aloud. There is no right or wrong way to do this.

'Close your eyes, now.
Let's take three deep breaths in and out together.
Bring your attention to focus on bravery.

I'm going to ask you a few questions, see what you notice as you answer these silently to yourself.

What colour would bravery be?

Does it have a shape?

If you could reach out and touch bravery, what would it feel like? It could be rough, smooth, furry, or flat.

What would its temperature be? Hot, cold, or warm?

Would it be big or small? Could you fit it in your hand or would it be larger?

Is it heavy or light?

Maybe bravery has a sound?

It could even have a movement. Fast or slow, steady, or pulsating.

Does it have a smell?

Would it have a taste?

Take a few moments to continue being curious about bravery. (Pause).

Letting your focus on bravery go now, knowing you can remember it anytime you need to.

Let's take three deep breaths in and out together.

Opening your eyes, coming back into this room.

Facilitator's top tip: You may ask the child/ren if there is anything they would like to share after the visualisation. Be curious about their experience and what stood out for them.

*****

Arriving Well Activity Book

Page title: Top tip # 2: Be approachable and smile.

Page no: 16

Page rationale: This page encourages 'the arriver' to adopt an inviting stance, increasing chances of connection by being approachable and smiling. Standing tall boosts confidence. Shifting the body into an upright position and bringing a smile to the face can positively impact internal physiology. The activity offers the opportunity for the child/ren to embody this attitude by role play, a chance to practise before they try it for real. Annotating the body outline helps increase the chances of the child adopting a welcoming stance.

Page visual:

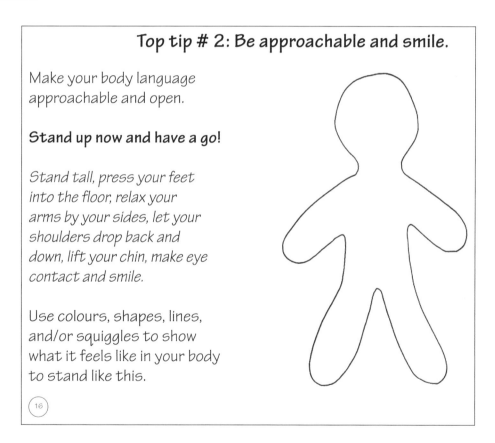

Materials needed: Each child needs: Pen, pencil, rubber, sharpener, coloured pens/pencils, activity book.

Setting the scene: You may say, *'Top tip number two is "Be approachable and smile".* *Standing tall, smiling, and making eye contact is a way to let others know you are* *approachable, friendly, and want to connect. This page gives you a chance to practise this with open body language'.*

Facilitator's top tip: The children may ask you what open body language is. You may say, *'When your body language is open, your body position and gestures show others you are up for talking to them and interested in making friends'.*

Completing the activity:

1) You may say, *'So, let's stand up and have a go!'*
2) Read through the instructions on the page, demonstrating it yourself.
3) In a group setting, ask the child/ren to walk around the room. Encourage eye contact. If you are supporting one child, practise this together.
4) Get the child/ren to return to their seats.
5) Bring their attention to the body outline on their page, let them know they are going to draw inside this. Invite them to use colours, shapes, lines, and/or squiggles to show what it felt like when they walked around the room with an approachable and friendly attitude.
6) You may say, *'Let's talk about what was happening inside of you when you were standing and moving around with open body language, where you felt it in your body, and the colours, shapes, lines, and/or squiggles you used to show this on your page'.* Invite responses.

Closure: You may say, *'Now you know how to be approachable and friendly, give it a go. Even if you don't feel completely confident, "fake it, till you make it". Every time you choose this attitude, you increase the chances of people noticing you and wanting to make friends'.*

*****

Arriving Well Activity Book

Page title: Top tip # 3: Keep curious. (Your new environment.)

Page no: 17

Page rationale: Neurological studies suggest the more inquisitive a child gets, the more they are willing to learn, discover, and explore. Furthermore, when curiosity is awakened, the brain floods the body with dopamine, increasing happiness (Fernandez Araoz, Roscoe, and Aramaki, 2018). These two findings are directly translatable to the process of transition. The next three pages draw on the adage that 'knowledge is power'. The child/ren will use their curiosity to discover information about their new place, which will boost confidence and aid settling.

Page visual:

Top tip # 3: Keep curious.

Your new environment.

Keep curious about your new environment by asking questions. Here are some examples:

- Where's the library?
- What's the best club to sign up for?
- What's the best thing to eat in the canteen?

Tell people about yourself but don't forget to find out about others. One thing everyone loves to talk about is themselves. Get curious about your new classmates.

Write down some questions you could ask new friends about themselves below:

Most likely, you'll have fewer friends at your new school to begin with. As life goes on, there will be ups and downs, more friends, less friends; one thing is for sure, life keeps changing.

17

Materials needed: Each child needs: Pen, pencil, rubber, sharpener, coloured pens/pencils, activity book.

Setting the scene: You may say, '*Top tip number three for moving out of "the dip" is "Keep curious". The next three pages will awaken your curiosity about your new place. An important part of curiosity is asking questions. So, on this page, you will be thinking about what questions you could ask to find out about your new environment*'.

Completing the activity:

1) Read the three questions that are written on their page – if they have already arrived in their new school, ask the child/ren if they know the answers to these. If they have not started their new school yet, highlight these as example questions to ask when they get there.

2) Ask if there are other important questions they'd like to consider. You may invite the child/ren to write these to the right of the three questions already listed on the page. Find a way of sharing their additional question ideas.

3) You may say, *'Most people like telling others about themselves. Using your curiosity by asking your new classmates questions is a great way to connect'*. Find a way to brainstorm questions to ask their peers; some examples might include, 'What do you like to do in your spare time?', 'How long have you lived here?', 'What's your favourite subject at school?

4) You may consider role-playing a classmate with the child/ren, inviting them to ask you some questions about yourself. In a group setting, consider pairing up the children, one role playing a peer, the other asking their 'peer' questions about themselves and swap over.

Facilitator's top tip: To make it as real as possible, if you are in a school setting, you may consider having an exisiting student visit the class, ready to be asked questions about themselves.

Closure: You may say, *'Most likely, at first, you will have fewer friends here than in your last place. That's normal, but getting curious about your new environment will help arrive well'*. If you are moving onto the next page, you might say, *'Let's continue with this theme of curiosity by getting curious about _____ (add new country name here)'*.

Extension activity: You may like to ask the children to experiment with asking some of the questions they thought of today and report back next time you meet.

*****

Arriving Well Activity Book

Page title: Top tip # 3: Keep curious. (New country report).

Page no: 18

Page rationale: This page invites the child to gather specific information about their new country. It is designed to foster curiosity and interest, helping 'the arriver' understand and connect to their new environment. It's offered in a playful way by the child/ren adopting a journalistic role.

Page visual:

Materials needed: Each child needs: Pen, pencil, rubber, sharpener, coloured pens/pencils, activity book.

Setting the scene: You may say, *'This page invites you to create a "new country report". You'll do this by filling in as many of the boxes on this page as you can. You will imagine you are a journalist (journalist means a reporter who is sharing interesting and important information). There are nine things to find out about. When this page is complete, you will know _____ (add name of new country) better than you did before; part of arriving well is becoming familiar with your new country'.*

Completing the activity:

1) Ask the child/ren to complete any of the boxes they already know the answer to.

Facilitator's top tip: If you are in a group setting, you may find a way to draw on the collective knowledge of the group.

2) You may like to invite the child/ren to research answers using devices, books, magazines, or leaflets.

Facilitator's top tip: If you feel the child/ren need more guidance, you may consider listing nine prospective answers on a white board (or equivalent). The children choose what they think is the correct answer for each box.

Facilitator's top tip: This may be a page you invite the children to complete in their own time. They can use devices/ask peers and/or adults as part of their research.

Closure: You may say, *'There is a well-known phrase that says "knowledge is power" – knowing as much as possible about _____ (add new country name here) will help you to feel settled and confident. This is just the beginning; there is much to learn and be discovered here'.*

Extension activity: Consider asking the child/ren what ideas they have of ways to present their research. They may be keen to create a journalistic vlog, blog, presentation, poster, or newspaper article about their findings.

*****

Arriving Well Activity Book

Page title: Top tip # 3: Keep curious. (Similarities and differences.)

Page no: 19

Page rationale: This page fosters curiosity of the similarities and differences between the last and new country. Engaging with both settings in this way creates balance and acceptance through curious reflection.

Page visual:

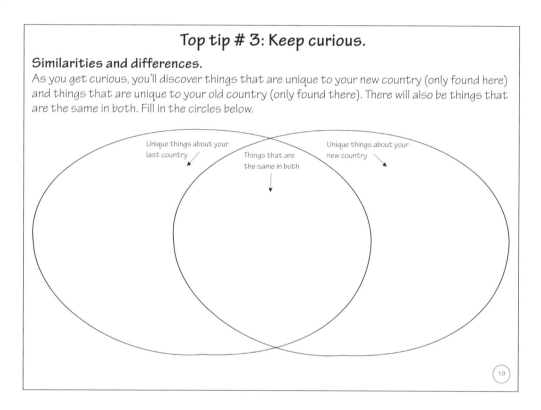

Materials needed: Each child needs: Pen, pencil, rubber, sharpener, coloured pens/pencils, activity book.

Setting the scene: You may say, *'As you get curious, you'll discover things that are unique to your new and old country and some things that are the same in both. This page is a Venn Diagram, which is way of presenting things that are different and the same about two things'.*

Completing the activity:

1) Begin by asking the child/ren to identify something that is unique (only found here) in their new place; pages 13 and 18 may help with this. Ask them to write their example in the right-hand section of the Venn diagram.

2) Next, ask the child/ren to think of one thing that is similar in the new and old place (almost the same in both); you might like to give some generic examples such as people drive and ride bikes, you can buy ice cream, there are walking paths to explore (make these fit your setting). Ask them to write their example in the middle section of the Venn diagram.

3) Lastly, ask the child/ren to think of something unique about their last country (things only found there); this could be to do with weather, language, clothes, or the flag. Ask them to write their example in the left-hand section of the Venn diagram.

4) Invite them to keep adding to any of the sections in which they can think of examples.

5) Find time for sharing of discoveries.

Closure: You may say, *'Just like us, countries are unique in their own way. Appreciating what's special about where you came from and where you are helps adopt a balanced view. When we remember the things that are similar in each place, it can help feel comfortable'.*

*****

Arriving Well Activity Book

Page title: Top tip # 4: Be yourself.

Page no: 20

Page rationale: Being genuine and authentic is vital to settle well. Being confident about who you are helps to build resilience and strength. This page asks the child to connect with five things they consider brilliant about themselves. The grey box at the bottom of the page highlights the value in taking opportunities and being open to trying new things.

Page visual:

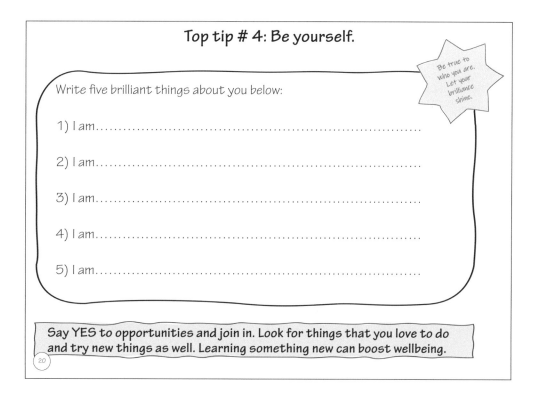

Materials needed: Each child needs: Pen, pencil, rubber, sharpener, coloured pens/pencils, activity book.

Setting the scene: You may say, *'Top tip number four is "Be yourself". This page asks you to think of five things that make you YOU. No two pages will be the same because we are all different. We'll talk about things you like to do; these activities are often an opportunity to be your best-self. We'll talk about trying new things too'.*

Completing the activity:

1) You may say, *'So, go ahead and begin making your list of five things that make you YOU. The list of five can be skills; things you are good at or positive things about your personality'.*

Facilitator's top tip: Feel free to give an example of five brilliant things you would write about you, if you feel comfortable doing so.

Facilitator's top tip: If a child is struggling to come up with things to write, you might like to give examples of things you have noticed they can include on their page or ask them what family members, friends, or teachers may say is wonderful about them.

2) You may say, *'When you are being yourself, you are genuine and real. People feel settled around those who are comfortable being themselves. This is an important list'.*
3) Let the child/ren know that when they are doing things they enjoy, they are often at their best. This may extend into a discussion of activities they engage in where they show their brilliance in their examples from 1–5.
4) You may say, *'Learning something new can boost wellbeing, can you think of anything new that you could learn or try in your time here?'* Invite responses.

Closure: You may say, *'Being yourself is an important part of arriving well. Remember, doing things that you love and trying new things helps to let your brilliance shine. If you need a confidence boost, return to this page and read your list.*

*****

Arriving Well Activity Book

Page title: Top tip # 5: Be kind. (Kind to others.)

Page no: 21

Page rationale: This page, based on the work of Martin Seligman, raises awareness that acts of kindness can benefit both the recipient and the person being kind. Being kind can help to arrive well; when a person carries out acts of kindness, feelings of confidence, being in control, happiness, and optimism can be boosted. Acts of kindness may also encourage others to repeat the good deeds they've experienced themselves, increasing the connectedness of the community.

Page visual:

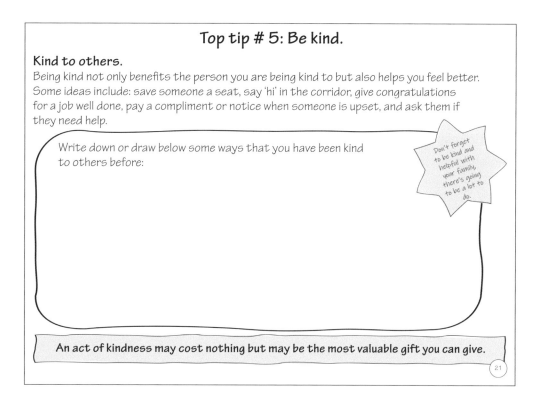

Materials needed: Each child needs: Pen, pencil, rubber, sharpener, coloured pens/pencils, activity book.

Setting the scene: You may say, *'Top tip number five for arriving well is "be kind". Being kind to others makes them feel better and boosts your wellbeing too; in fact, the whole community feels more connected when there is more kindness about'.*

Completing the activity:

1) Read through the examples in the top paragraph of the page. Ask the child/ren if they can think of other ways of being kind.

2) Highlight the grey star. You may say, *'Arriving and settling is challenging for the whole family. Offering kindness to your family members will help you all settle more smoothly'*.

3) Invite the child/ren to reflect on past acts of kindness. Ask them to add ways they have been kind to others inside the big rectangle on their page.

4) Find a way for the child/ren to share. In a group setting, they can get ideas of ways to be kind from each other.

Facilitator's top tip: You might like to ask the child/ren if they can think of a time that someone has been kind to them and ask them how that made them feel.

Closure: You may say, *'Acts of kindness don't cost anything, but it may be the most valuable gift you can give. I'm going to invite you to try an experiment, a kindness challenge, if you like. Everyday offer an act of kindness to someone. Next time when we meet, you can report back on what you discovered'*.

Extension activity: You may like to deliver pages 21 and 22 in one session. If you do, there is a '7-day kindness challenge' worksheet included in page 22's Extension activity you can share. It includes the task above and another from page 22.

*****

Arriving Well Activity Book

Page title: Top tip # 5: Be kind. (Kind to self.)

Page no: 22

Page rationale: Self-kindness is a positive, proactive attitude towards oneself. Most of us are good at being kind to others. Self-kindness turns this practice inwards; we treat ourselves as kindly as we would a good friend. This page takes inspiration from the work of Kristin Neff who is well known for her work on self-compassion. She highlights that being kind to oneself has been proven to boost wellbeing, resilience, optimism, and social connectedness. This page encourages the child to make choices that are intentionally kind to themselves during this settling phase.

Page visual:

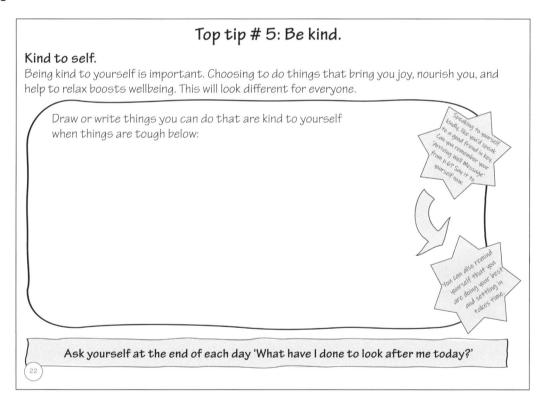

Materials needed: Each child needs: Pen, pencil, rubber, sharpener, coloured pens/pencils, activity book, additional worksheet included in the Extension activity of this page as needed.

Setting the scene: You may say, *'This page continues with the theme of kindness. Most of us find being kind to others easy but being kind to yourself is more difficult. It's easy* to forget about, especially when life gets busy. Making a choice to do things you enjoy, things that help you relax, and speaking kindly to yourself are all important parts of being kind to you'.

Completing the activity:

1) You may like to begin this activity by leading one of the regulation techniques shared on pages 7 and 8 of this activity book. After completing, highlight that slowing down is a way of being kind to yourself; doing so helps make good choices.

Facilitator's top tip: You may choose to lead your own breathing/grounding technique if you wish.

2) You may say, *'Let's think about things you can do that are kind to yourself; these are things that help relax and nourish you. When things nourish you, they lift your mood, bring you joy, help you recover when things are tough, boost wellbeing, and help you feel positive. Things people choose to do to relax and nourish themselves vary from person to person'.*

3) Invite the child/ren to write or draw things they can do to be kind to themselves in the big rectangle on their page. You may like to give some examples of ways you are kind to yourself. Or you may like to give some examples of things children might say, for example, 'Go for a bike ride', 'Play with my dog', 'Hang out with my friend', 'Do some colouring', 'Make something', 'Listen to relaxing music', 'Playing my recorder', 'Draw a picture', 'Write a poem', 'Take some deep breaths'.

4) Find a way for sharing ideas and suggestions, highlighting that we can learn from each other.

5) You may say, *'It's not only our actions that can be kind to ourselves but also our thinking. An important part of being kind to you is speaking kindly in your mind. Speak to yourself as you would a good friend'.*

Facilitator's top tip: You may like to add, *'Sometimes when things are challenging, it's not easy to think of kind things to say to yourself. If this happens, take a breath and ask yourself what your good friend might say'.*

6) Invite the children to turn to page 6 and read their 'Arriving Well Message' to themselves now.

7) Bring them back to page 22. You may say, *'It might help to remember your message from time to time and that settling in takes a while. Remind yourself you are doing your best. The grey star at the bottom right of your page reminds you of this'.*

Closure: You may say, *'Being kind to yourself is not an easy task; try your best to do this until we meet again. A helpful way to reflect, at the end of each day might be, to ask yourself, "What have I done to look after me today?" Think of this as your very own kindness challenge'.*

Extension activity: You may like to photocopy (enlarge as required) the '7-day kindness challenge' below for the child/ren to take away to record on each day (which includes the challenge from page 21 too).

Kindness challenge:

Arriving Well Activity Book

Page title: Top tip # 6: Be grateful.

Page no: 23

Page rationale: Gratitude is the act of recognising and acknowledging good things that happen, resulting in a state of appreciation. Martin Seligman, a world-renowned psychologist, states that expressing gratitude can positively impact wellbeing. This page introduces gratitude, inviting an intentional practice of noticing three things that the child is grateful for. The intention is for gratitude to awaken and grow within the child, helping them arrive well.

Page visual:

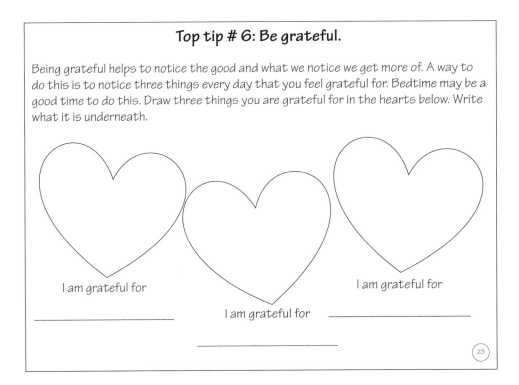

Materials needed: Each child needs: Pen, pencil, rubber, sharpener, coloured pens/pencils, activity book, scrap paper as needed.

Setting the scene: You may say, *'Top tip number six is "Be grateful". Being grateful is about noticing good things in life and appreciating them. When we pay attention to good things,* *the more good things we notice. Being grateful boosts wellbeing, making "arriving well" more manageable'.*

Completing the activity:

1) You may like to begin this page by setting a timer for 1 minute and ask the child/ren to write down or share verbally things they are grateful for (they could use their brain dump on page 35 or a piece of scrap paper).
2) Invite the child/ren to choose the top three things they are grateful for.
3) Now, ask the child/ren to draw each of these, one in each of the hearts on their page. Then, write what it is underneath, on the line.
4) If you have time, find a way for the child/ren to share their top three.

Facilitator's top tip: If the child/ren are struggling to think of examples – give some of your own, or examples of what other children of their age might be grateful for.

Closure: You may say, *'Now your hearts are full, and you have practised your gratefulness, I'm going to give you a challenge to think of three things that you are grateful for everyday until we meet again. You can do this silently in your mind, say them out loud, or find a place to record them. It helps to do this at the same time each day to remember to do it; before bed works for some people, others like to do it as soon as they wake up. Doing this can boost wellbeing, I'm curious to see how it might be helpful for we until we meet again'.*

Facilitator's top tip: You may choose to copy and share the Gratitiude challenge included in the Extension activity below for the child/ren to record the three things they are grateful for each day.

Extension activity: You may like to invite the child/ren to think of someone whom they feel a sense of gratitude towards and write them a letter about what they appreciate. This can be even more powerful if the child/ren read their letter to the person they wrote it to.

A simpler, quicker version of this is to give each child a post-it note and ask them to write a short message saying why they feel grateful to a particular person. Invite them to give the post-it note to the person, if possible.

Gratitude challenge:

Gratitude Challenge

Day 1:

Day 2:

Day 3:

Day 4:

Day 5:

Day 6:

Day 7:

*****

Arriving Well Activity Book

Page title: Top tip # 7: Focus on your strengths. (What are strengths?)

Page no: 24

Page rationale: Knowing and acknowledging one's strengths boosts self-esteem. When we appreciate our positive character traits, we feel more confident and capable. This lifts wellbeing and allows us to be the best version of ourselves. This page introduces the idea of focusing on strengths and builds strength-based vocabulary.

Page visual:

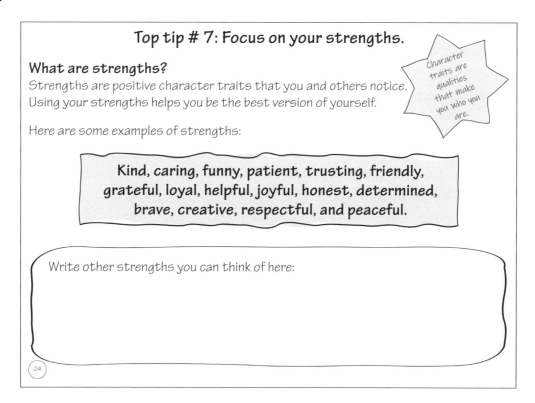

Materials needed: Each child needs: Pen, pencil, rubber, sharpener, coloured pens/pencils, activity book.

Setting the scene: You may say, *'Top tip number seven is "Focus on your strengths". Strengths are positive character traits you and others notice. Character traits are qualities that make you who you are. Using your strengths helps be the best version of yourself and boosts wellbeing'.*

Facilitator's top tip: Pages 24 and 25 lend themselves to being delivered in the same session.

Completing the activity:

1) Read through the examples of strengths listed on the page in the grey box.
2) Invite the child/ren to add others they can think of in the box at the bottom of the page.
3) Give each child a blank piece of paper. Invite them to write their name at the top. If you are working with one child, create one for you as well. If you are in a group setting, each child should have a piece of paper with their name on.
4) You may say, *'This activity invites you to write strengths of the person whose name is on the paper'.*
5) You can facilitate this by swapping papers around the group (or between you if you are supporting one child) or sticking the paper to the persons back whose name is on the paper and strengths are added to the paper whilst the page is on their back.
6) Whichever way you choose, at the end of the activity, invite the child whose name is on the paper to add a strength they appreciate in themselves to their own paper.
7) Invite child/ren to read through their list. You may like to ask, *'Which strength do you think you have lots of?'* Ask them to share and say why.

Facilitator's top tip: The child/ren will need their list for the activity on the next page.

Closure: You may say, *'The cool thing about strengths is that they are always within you, ready to help you be the best version of yourself'.*

Extension activity: Ask the child/ren to notice times they are using their strengths and when they notice strengths in others.

*****

Arriving Well Activity Book

Page title: Top tip # 7: Focus on your strengths. (Strengths that you take everywhere you go.)

Page no: 25

Page rationale: This page invites acknowledgement of strengths and encourages the child/ren to think about them in relation to transition. We all have signature strengths (these are character traits that we find easy to practise and show others) and growth strengths (those that we can grow more if we need to call upon them for certain situations). The activities presented promote reflection on these in relation to arriving well.

Page visual:

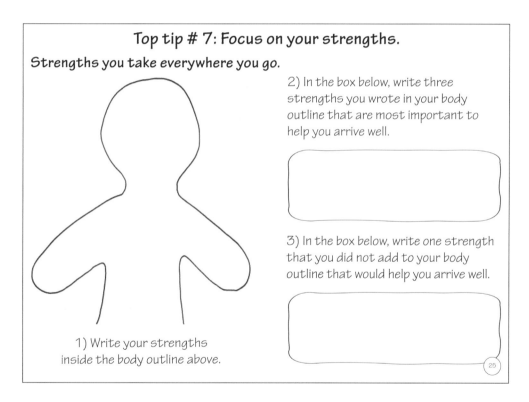

Materials needed: Each child needs: Pen, pencil, rubber, sharpener, coloured pens/pencils, activity book.

Setting the scene: You may say, *'This page carries on from the last, you are going to keep thinking about your strengths'.*

Completing the activity:

1) Begin by telling the child/ren they need their strength list generated from the last page's activity.
2) Transfer the list to this page, writing the strengths inside the body outline.
3) Invite them to add any others they think should be included.
4) You may say, *'The strengths you have written inside your body outline can be called your "signature strengths". These are the ones that you find easily and others notice them too'.*
5) Next, move to 2) on the page. Invite the child/ren to choose three of their signature strengths they wrote in their body outline that will help arrive well.
6) You may say, *'We also have growth strengths. These are the strengths that are a little harder to find, maybe they don't come as naturally as your signature strengths. At times of change, awakening our growth strengths might help settle. Look at task number 3 on your page; can you think of a strength you didn't add to your body outline but one that would be good to grow more of during this transition?'*

Facilitator's top tip: You might share a list of strengths with the child/ren for 6) above.

7) Invite the child/ren to add their growth strength to the box on the bottom right of their page.
8) Find a way for the children to share their discoveries. If you are supporting one child, be curious about what they have written in the body outline and the two boxes. You may ask them what made them choose their three strengths they wrote in box 2). You may ask what they need to do more of or less of to develop the strengths they wrote in box 3). In a group setting, you might also like to propose these questions or a simple sharing; each child may share 'My three signature strengths that will help me arrive well are _____, my growth strength that will help me arrive well is _____'.

Closure: You may say, *'Now you've got to know your strengths. It's time to start noticing yourself using them. You can think of your strengths as your superpowers you take everywhere you go'.*

*****

Arriving Well Activity Book

Page title: Top tip # 8: Remember your old place.

Page no: 26

Page rationale: Some children try to forget about their last place; recalling it might feel painful. This page honours that arriving well involves acknowledging what can be celebrated from the previous setting and that maintaining meaningful relationships is important. Positive experiences in the last place may hold some important information for settling in the new setting. Striking a balance between remembering the last place and making the most of the new place helps to arrive well.

Page visual:

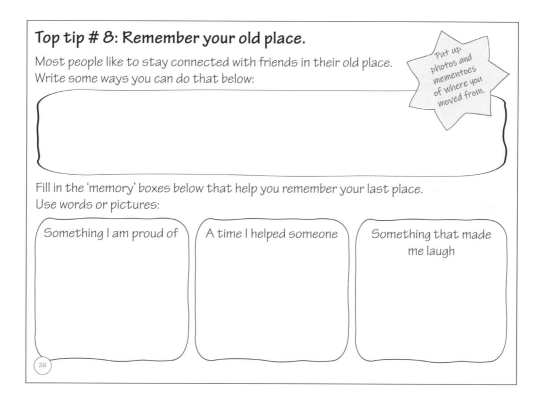

Materials needed: Each child needs: Pen, pencil, rubber, sharpener, coloured pens/pencils, activity book.

Setting the scene: You may say, *'Top tip number eight is "Remember your old place". We've talked about making new connections. This is important to arrive well but remembering your old place and maintaining relationships there is important too'.*

Completing the activity:

1) You may say, *'There are a few ways you can stay connected with important people in your last country. Write some ways you can do this in the box at the top of the page'.*

2) Bring the child/ren's attention to the grey star at the top right of the page. Read it out loud or ask the children to read it silently to themselves. Check their understanding of the word mementoes. You may say, *'Mementoes are special items from your old place like souvenirs, keepsakes, certificates, medals, and the like'*. Highlight these things can be a great way of fondly remembering their previous setting.

3) Bring the child/ren's attention to the 'memory boxes' at the bottom of the page. You may say, *'Memories of positive times and things that went well in the old place are important to hold dear to help arrive well'*. Invite the child/ren to fill the memory boxes.

4) Find an appropriate way for sharing their memory boxes.

Closure: You may say, *'Remembering your old place holds some important clues and information for settling well. What worked there may be the key to success here. Chances are, you may well see those special people whom you keep in touch with again. Have you heard the expression 'The world is a small place'? It means that it's not unusual to meet people again'.*

*****

Arriving Well Activity Book

Page title: Top tip # 9: Make your bedroom a haven.

Page no: 27

Page rationale: Having a physical safe space creates a sense of psychological safety. On moving to a new country, having a place that feels protective and comfortable helps to feel grounded and rooted. Setting up or identifying a safe space to regulate and retreat to, as needed, is an important part of an 'arrivers' self-care provision.

Page visual:

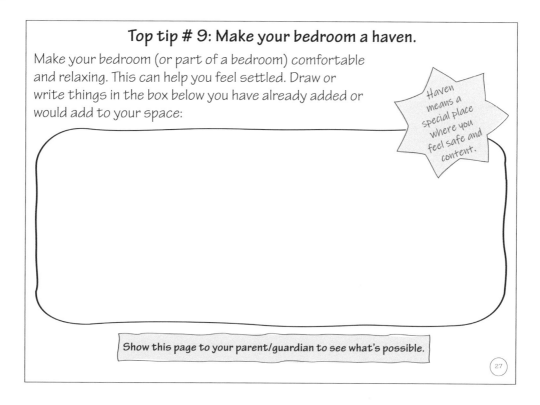

Materials needed: Each child needs: Pen, pencil, rubber, sharpener, coloured pens/pencils, activity book.

Setting the scene: You may say, *'Top tip number nine is "Make your bedroom your haven". Having a place where you can feel safe and comfortable helps to arrive well. This can be a place where you can be calm and relaxed and a spot where you can boost your wellbeing as needed. Your bedroom, or part of a bedroom, is an ideal spot to create your "haven". As you can see in the star on the page, "haven" means a special place where you feel safe and content'.*

Completing the activity:

1) You may say, *'This activity is a bit like creating a mood-board, a creative plan for constructing your haven'*.

2) You may say, *'You may have already made a space at home feel like a haven, perhaps you bought some special things with you that help create a calming space. If so, write or draw these things in the box on your page. If not, start from scratch. It's time to dream calmness and get creative. Keep adding items you'd like to include'*.

3) As the child/ren are working on their page, invite them to think about colours, lighting, sounds, all important components of a relaxing environment.

Facilitator's top tip: You might like to have some catalogues/magazines for them to cut out images or take inspirtaion from. You may invite them to source online images for the same purpose.

Closure: As teachers/therapists, you may say, *'I feel calmer, seeing you generate ideas for your haven/s. Remember when you plan things, they don't always turn out as you think they will; do talk to you parents or guardians about what might be possible in your space, explain why the things you chose are important to you. When you have created your haven, take some time to relax there. It may become a place you visit to steady yourself when big feelings arrive using things we have talked about in this activity book'*. Parents may say, *'I feel calmer, seeing you generate ideas for your haven/s. I'm here to help you get it set up. When you have created your haven, take some time to relax there. It may become a place you visit to steady yourself when big feelings arrive using things we have talked about in this activity book'*.

Extension activity: You may invite the child/ren to discuss helpful things they would do in their haven. You may ask them to create a poster for their wall with a reminder of some ways they can boost wellbeing whilst in their haven. Examples may include listening to music, drawing, mindful colouring, writing, doing something kind for themselves, speaking to someone online or face to face, playing an instrument, being grateful, thinking about their strengths, a grounding activity like 54321, a breathing activity like Mountain Breathing, and/or telling themselves something positive like their 'Arriving Well Message'.

*****

Arriving Well Activity Book

Page title: Top tip # 10: Ask for help.

Page no: 28

Page rationale: Identifying a circle of support which contains people who can be called upon in times of need helps to feel safe. Naming supportive people ahead of time increases the chances of being able to call on them when help is required. This page encourages the child/ren to think of three 'helpers' (and more if they choose) who they could ask for support when the going gets tough.

Page visual:

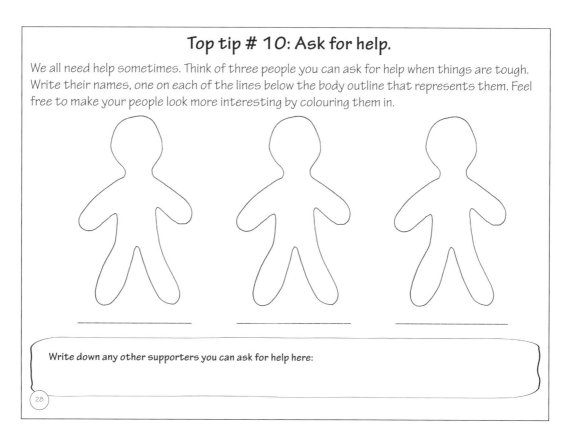

Materials needed: Each child needs: Pen, pencil, rubber, sharpener, coloured pens/pencils, activity book, scissors, paper people worksheet included in the Extension activity of this page as needed.

Setting the scene: You may say, *'Top tip number ten is "Ask for help". Moving to a new country is challenging, we all need a bit of extra help from people around us at times of transition. Thinking about who that might be beforehand can increase the chances of you reaching out to them in times of need'.*

Completing the activity:

1) You may say, *'Think of three people you could ask for help. The three body outlines on your page represent each of these people. Write their names underneath their body outline on the line provided'.*
2) You may say, *'Let's get creative by bringing each of your people to life on your page. Colour in each of the people in a way that reminds you of who they are'.*
3) You may say, *'It may be that there are more people you can think of to ask for help from if you need it. Write their names in the rectangular box at the bottom of the page'.*

Facilitator's top tip: If the child/ren are having a hard time thinking of three people, highlight these could be yourself, family members, siblings, friends, peers, teachers, or other people in their community. They may even be people from their last setting. You may like to give examples from other child/ren's pages if you are in a group setting. You may share who you would name as your three supporters.

Closure: You may say, *'You've literally got your supportive people in front of you as you look at your page; remember everyone asks for help sometimes. When settling in a new place, it's likely you are going to need more help than usual'.*

Extension activity: If time allows, extract more information from the child/ren by inviting them to think of what each person would be able to help with and how they would know it was time to contact them.

Facilitator's top tip: You may like to extend this activity by inviting the child/ren to bring their supporters to life by making a people paper chain.

People paper chain: Creating a people paper chain could be done with you facilitating or the child/ren may complete in their own time. If you are facilitating read out the instructions step by step to the child/ren.

1) Print the paper people sheet below, enlarge as desired:

2) Cut along all dotted lines so that you have two rectangles and two paper people templates.
3) Take one of the templates and fold all the solid lines, into four sections, making sure the person outline can be seen on the top.
4) Carefully cut out the person outline, cutting through all the layers of folded paper. BE SURE TO LEAVE THE HANDS INTACT!
5) Carefully unfold to see your paper people chain.

Encourage the children to colour their people and consider putting them up somewhere; they will see them often to remind them of who to ask for help.

*****

Arriving Well Activity Book

Page title: Moving on podium.

Page no: 29

Page rationale: This closure and integration activity helps children reflect on what stood out for them from the *Arriving Well Activity Book*. It helps pull out pertinent learning and cements engagement with the text.

Page visual:

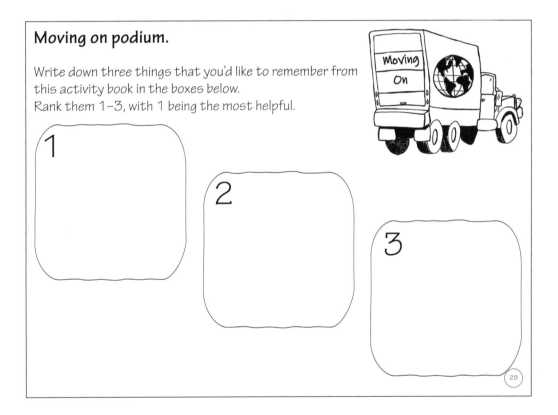

Materials needed: Each child needs: Pen, pencil, rubber, sharpener, coloured pens/pencils, activity book.

Setting the scene: You may say, *'As we draw closer to the end of the book, you are going to recall what you'd most like to remember. It's a bit like finishing a sports event. You might have seen a podium where the best competitors stand at the end. Maybe you've stood on one of these yourself? This page invites you to place on your podium the most important things you want to remember from this activity book'*.

Completing the activity:

1) Feel free to offer a summary of things you have covered in the *Arriving Well Activity Book*.

Facilitator's top tip: You may ask the children to close their eyes as you recount things covered in your time together. This may help them recall what's been important for them.

2) Ask the child/ren to identify three things they'd like to remember and rank them 1–3, with 1 being the most important, and write them on their podium in the respective boxes. You may like to offer scrap paper for them to make their rough list first.
3) Find a way for sharing of podiums.

Closure: You may say, *'Everyone's podium is different, just like every person and their journey is different. Thank you for thinking so carefully about yours and what you'd like to remember from the* Arriving Well Activity Book.*'*

*****

Arriving Well Activity Book

Page title: Instructions for making a 'Wellbeing Boost Game'.

Page no: 30

Page rationale: This page details the instructions for the Wellbeing Boost Game on page 31.

Page visual:

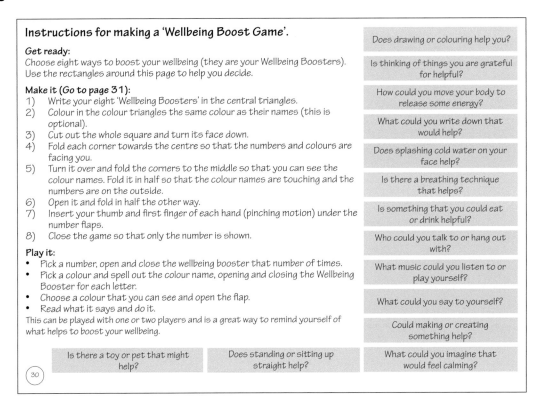

Materials needed: Each child needs: Pen, pencil, rubber, sharpener, coloured pens/pencils, activity book, extra paper as needed.

Setting the scene: You may say, *'We are going to make a game you can play called Wellbeing Boost Game. It's a way to help you choose a wellbeing strategy at times when you need to steady yourself'.*

Completing the activity:

1) You may say, *'Before you make your game, you'll need to choose eight ways you can boost wellbeing; these are your "wellbeing boosters". Remember everyone is unique and will choose different boosters'.*

2) You may say, *'Go ahead and choose eight wellbeing boosters for yourself. Have a look at the questions in the grey boxes to help you decide on your eight'*.

3) Invite the children to write these on their 'brain-dump' box on page 35.

Facilitator's top tip: If the child/ren's brain-dump page is full or you prefer to, give them an additonal piece of paper to list their eight wellbeing boosters.

Facilitator's top tip: Some children will find it easier than others to create their list. If a child is struggling, you might like to guide them more carefully through questions in the grey boxes or ask them what strategies they remember from the *Arriving Well Activity Book*. Flick through the book together as needed. You might like to ask them, *'Can you think of a time when you were feeling overwhelmed and you did something that helped you feel better? What was it that you did?'*

If you are in a group, you might like to ask a child who has chosen their eight wellbeing boosters to share their's with the group to help those who need a few more ideas.

Closure: You may say, *'So, now you have your eight wellbeing boosters, you can start making your game. Let's turn to page 31 to begin'*.

*****

Arriving Well Activity Book

Page title: Wellbeing Boost Game.

Page no: 31

Page rationale: This playful integration activity brings together regulation strategies shared in the *Arriving Well Activity Book*. Making the game encourages the child to identify the most helpful coping strategies and reminds them that they can make good choices for themselves in moments of overwhelm.

Page visual:

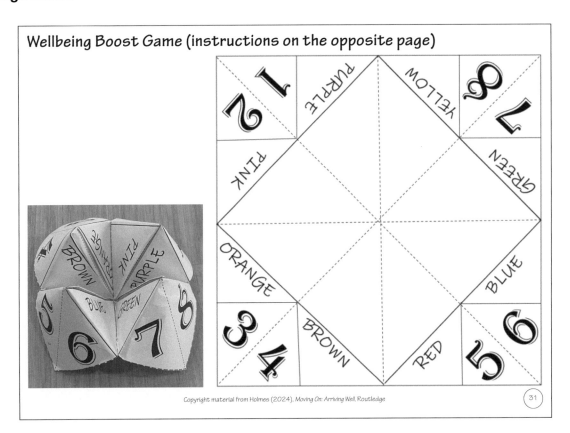

Wellbeing Boost Game (instructions on the opposite page)

Materials needed: Each child needs: Pen, pencil, rubber, sharpener, coloured pens/pencils, scissors, activity book, scissors.

Setting the scene: Ask the child/ren if they are ready to start making their 'Wellbeing Boost Game'. You may say, *'When it's finished, this game can be used for a bit of fun and at times when you feel stressed, it will help you choose a strategy to boost wellbeing when you need it'.*

Facilitator's top tip: As facilitator, you may like to refer to the instructions on page 30 of the *Arriving Well Activity Book* to help you guide the child/ren. It may help to have a completed game to show the child/ren to help visualise what they are creating and/or to demonstrate the folding and cutting procedures with a blank 'Wellbeing Boost Game' template (feel free to copy and enlarge the page visual above for this purpose).

Completing the activity:

1) Work through the eight instructions in the 'Make it' section on page 30.

Facilitator's top tip: Some children may prefer to draw pictures, rather than write on their game. Offer this option if you think it helpful.

2) Guide the child/ren though the 'Play it' section on page 30. You may like to invite them to try it out on their own, with a partner or with you.

Facilitator's top tip: Offer as much help as is needed in the construction phase of the 'Wellbeing Boost Game' creation. For some, the cutting out and/or the making the game itself might be challenging.

Closure: You may say: '*So, now you have your "Wellbeing Boost Game" to select a coping strategy at a time when you need it. I look forward to hearing about time it helped you*'.

*****

Arriving Well Activity Book

Page title: Awards Ceremony.

Page no: 33

Page rationale: This closure and integration activity invites the child/ren reflect on their experience with the *Arriving Well Activity Book*. It helps pull out pertinent learning and appreciate efforts of engagement with the material.

Page visual:

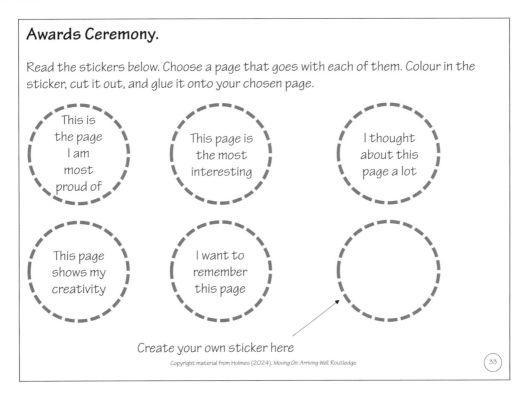

Materials needed: Each child needs: Pen, pencil, rubber, sharpener, coloured pens/pencils, activity book, scissors, and glue.

Setting the scene: You may say. *'You have worked hard to complete the pages of the* Arriving Well Activity Book. *Now, it's time to give some self-appreciation by giving yourself six awards'.*

Completing the activity:

1) Invite the children to read through the awards on the page silently or you may choose to read them aloud.
2) Ask the children to colour in each of the stickers.

3) Invite them to write an additional award they would like to give themselves in the blank circle if they wish.

4) Next, ask the child/ren to cut out the stickers and place them in front of them.

5) Invite them to choose a sticker, match it to their chosen page, and stick it in. Repeat with the remaining five stickers.

6) Ask the child/ren to show you, or a partner which sticker they placed on which page and say as little or as much as they would like about that.

Facilitator's top tip: Assist the child/ren as necessary with cutting out the stickers.

Closure: You may say, *'Notice how it feels to acknowledge your hard work. It's been great to see you do this and hear which pages you appreciate most'*.

Congratulate the child/ren on their completion of the pages of this activity book. Let them know that you hope their learnings will help them with the next stage of their adventure.

A big well done to you too for supporting the child/ren journey through the *Arriving Well Activity Book*.

*****

Arriving Well Activity Book

Page title: 'Brain-dump page'.

Page no: 35

Page rationale: This page is a versatile space for the child/ren to make notes and/or plan. Facilitators are encouraged to use this page as they see fit.

Page visual:

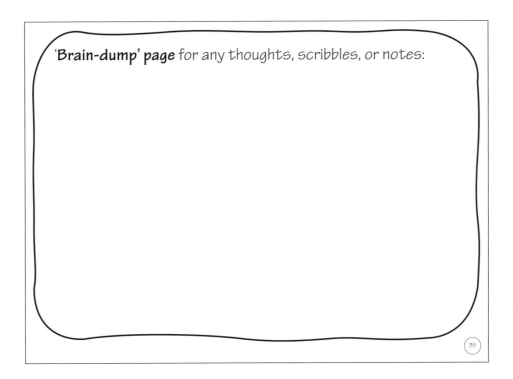

'Brain-dump' page for any thoughts, scribbles, or notes:

35

*****

Bibliography

Fernandez Araoz, C., Roscoe, A. and Aramaki, K., 2018. From curious to competent. *Harvard Business Review*, 96(5), p.61.

Lysgaard, S., 1955. Adjustment in a foreign society: Norwegian Fulbright grantees visiting the United States. International Social Science Bulletin, 7, 45–51. *Journal of Counseling Psychology*, 53(1), pp.126–131.

Mahler, K., 2019. *The interoception curriculum: A step-by-step framework for developing mindful self-regulation*. Hershey, PA: Kelly Mahler.

Neff, K., 2011. *Self-compassion: The proven power of being kind to yourself*. New York, NY: Harper-Collins Publishers.

Ota, D.W., 2014. *Safe passage how mobility affects people & what international schools should do about it*. Stamford, CT: Summertime Publishing.

Pollock, D.C., Van Reken, R.E. and Pollock, M.V., 2017. *Third culture kids: Growing up among worlds*. Boston, MA: Nicholas Brealey Publishing.

Seligman, M.E.P., 2002. *Authentic happiness: Using the new positive psychology to realize your potential for lasting fulfilment*. London: Nicholas Brealey Publishing.

Seligman, M.E.P., 2012. *Flourish: A visionary new understanding of happiness and well-being*. New York, NY: Atria Paperback.

Siegel, D.J. and Bryson, T.P., 2012. *The whole-brain child: 12 revolutionary strategies to nurture your child's developing mind*. New York, NY: Bantam Books.

Index

and there's more 27–28; closure 28; completing the activity 28; extension activity 28; materials needed 27; page rationale 27; page visual 27; setting the scene 27

Arriving Well Activity Book 119–121; asking for help 133–135; awards ceremony 142–143; being approachable and smile 107–108; being brave 104–106; being grateful 122–124; being kind (kind to others) 117–118; being kind (kind to self) 119–121; being yourself 115–116; brain-dump page 144; feelings wheel 83–84; focus on your strengths (strengths that you take everywhere you go) 127–128; focus on your strengths (What are strengths?) 125–126; ground oneself 89–90; instructions for making a 'Wellbeing Boost Game' 138–139; It's wonderful and new 100–101; keeping curious (new country report) 111–112; keeping curious (similarities and differences) 113–114; keeping curious (your new environment) 109–110; keep your breath in mind 87–88; listen to your body and speak kindly to yourself 85–86; making your bedroom a haven 131–132; mindful colouring 95–96; missing where you came from 102–103; move your body to lift your mood 97–99; moving on graph 91–92; moving on podium 136–137; pros (things that are good) and cons (things that are not so good) 93–94; remember your old place 129–130; welcome 76–77; Wellbeing Boost Game 140–141

asking for help 133–135; closure 134; completing the activity 134; extension activity 134; facilitators tip 134; materials needed 133; page rationale 133; page visual 133; people paper chain 135; setting the scene 134

awards ceremony 72–73, 142–143; closure 73; completing the activity 72–73, 142–143; facilitators tip 73; materials needed 72, 142; page rationale 72, 142; page visual 72, 142; setting the scene 72, 142

ballooning around 62–63; closure 63; completing the activity 63; facilitators tip 63; materials needed 62; page rationale 62; page visual 62; setting the scene 62

being approachable and smile 107–108; closure 108; completing the activity 108; facilitators tip 108; materials needed 107; page rationale 107; page visual 107; setting the scene 107–108

being brave 104–106; closure 105; completing the activity 105; exploring bravery visualisation 105–106; extension activity 105; facilitators tip 105, 106; materials needed 104; page rationale 104; page visual 104; setting the scene 104

being grateful 122–124; closure 123; completing the activity 123; extension activity 123; facilitators tip 123; gratitude challenge 124; materials needed 122; page rationale 122; page visual 122; setting the scene 122–123

being kind (kind to others) 117–118; closure 118; completing the activity 118; extension activity 118; facilitators tip 118; materials needed 117; page rationale 117; page visual 117; setting the scene 117

being kind (kind to self) 119–121; closure 121; completing the activity 120; extension activity 121; facilitators tip 120; kindness challenge 121; materials needed 119; page rationale 119; page visual 119; setting the scene 119–120

being yourself 115–116; closure 116; completing the activity 116; facilitators tip 116; materials needed 115; page rationale 115; page visual 115; setting the scene 115

brain-dump page 67; page rationale 144; page visual 144

change happens 6–7; closure 7; completing the activity 7; facilitators tip 7; materials needed 6; page rationale 6; page visual 6; setting the scene 6

coping cube 70–71; closure 71; completing the activity 71; extension activity 71; facilitators tip 70–71; materials needed 70; page rationale 70; page visual 70; setting the scene 70

culture shock 102

curiouser and curiouser… 60–61; closure 61; completing the activity 61; extension activity 61; facilitators tip 61; materials needed 60; page rationale 60; page visual 60; setting the scene 60

draw feelings out 22–24; closure 24; completing the activity 23; exploring a feeling visualisation 23–24; extension activity 24; facilitators tip 22–24; materials needed 22; page rationale 22; page visual 22; setting the scene 22

feelings faces 19–21; closure 21; completing the activity 20; facilitators tip 20–21; materials needed 19; page rationale 19; page visual 19; setting the scene 20

feelings wheel 83–84; closure 84; completing the activity 84; facilitators tip 84; materials needed 83; page rationale 83; page visual 83; setting the scene 83

54321 (practice) 89–90

focus on your strengths (strengths that you take everywhere you go) 127–128; closure 128; completing the activity 128; facilitators tip 128; materials needed 127; page rationale 127; page visual 127; setting the scene 127

focus on your strengths (What are strengths?) 125–126; closure 126; completing the activity 126; extension activity 126; facilitators tip 125, 126; materials needed 125; page rationale 125; page visual 125; setting the scene 125

gallery of strengths 64–65; closure 65; completing the activity 64–65; facilitators tip 65; materials needed 64; page rationale 64; page visual 64; setting the scene 64

getting curious 58–59; closure 59; completing the activity 59; extension activity 59; facilitators tip 59; materials needed 58; page rationale 58; page visual 58; setting the scene 58

ground oneself 89–90; closure 90; completing the activity 90; extension activity 90; facilitators tip 90; materials needed 89; page rationale 89; page visual 89; setting the scene 89

GUTS[2] model 10–11, 12–13, 19, 20, 33, 37, 59; closure 11; completing the activity 11; extension activity 11; materials needed 10; page rationale 10; page visual 10; setting the scene 10

hope and fears flower 29–31; closure 31; completing the activity 30; extension activity 31; facilitators tip 30; materials needed 29; page rationale 29; page visual 29; setting the scene 29

how do I cope well? 40–42; closure 41; completing the activity 41; extension activity 41; facilitators tip 41, 42; materials needed 40; page rationale 40; page visual 40; safe space visualisation 41–42; setting the scene 40 inner coach 44

inner critic 44

instructions for making a 'Wellbeing Boost Game' 138–139; closure 139; completing the activity 138–139; facilitators tip 139; materials needed 138; page rationale 138; page visual 138; setting the scene 138

It's wonderful and new 100–101; closure 101; completing the activity 101; facilitators tip 101; materials needed 100; page rationale 100; page visual 100; setting the scene 100

keeping curious (new country report) 111–112; closure 112; completing the activity 112; extension activity 112; facilitators tip 112; materials needed 111; page rationale 111; page visual 111; setting the scene 111

keeping curious (similarities and differences) 113–114; closure 114; completing the activity 114; materials needed 113; page rationale 113; page visual 113; setting the scene 113

keeping curious (your new environment) 109–110; closure 110; completing the activity 110; extension activity 110; facilitators tip 110; materials needed 109; page rationale 109; page visual 109; setting the scene 109

keep your breath in mind 87–88; closure 88; completing the activity 88; extension activity 88; facilitators tip 88; materials needed 87; page rationale 87; page visual 87; setting the scene 87

leaving things behind 14–15; closure 15; completing the activity 15; materials needed 14; page rationale 14; page visual 14; setting the scene 14

Leaving Well Activity Book 68–69; awards ceremony 72–73; ballooning around 62–63; change happens 6–7; coping cube 70–71; curiouser and curiouser… 60–61; draw feelings out 22–24; feelings faces 19–21; gallery of strengths 64–65; getting curious 58–59; hope and fears flower 29–31; how do I cope well? 40–42; leaving things behind 14–15; lighten the load 16–18; moving on graph 8–9; moving on podium 68–69; moving on poem 66–67; moving on takes GUTS[2] 10–11; my well-wishes 74–75; people power 12–13; stand like a tree 55–57; staying connected 34–35; take 5 50–51; talk feelings out 25–26; thankfulness tree 52–54; and there's more 27–28; welcome 1–3; what brings me joy? 36–37; what does my body tell me? 38–39; what encouraging things can I say to myself? 43–44; what's in and out of my control? 45–47; where are you now? 4–5; who and how? 32–33

lighten the load 16–18; closure 17–18; completing the activity 17; extension activity 18; facilitators tip 17; materials needed 16; page rationale 16; page visual 16; setting the scene 16

listen to your body and speak kindly to yourself 85–86; closure 86; completing the activity 86; extension activity 86; facilitators tip 86; materials needed 85; page rationale 85; page visual 85; setting the scene 85

Lysgaard, Sverre 91

Mahler, Kelly 38

making your bedroom a haven 131–132; closure 132; completing the activity 132; extension activity 132; facilitators tip 132; materials needed 131; page rationale 131; page visual 131; setting the scene 131

mementoes 130

mindful colouring 48–49, 95–96; closure 49, 96; completing the activity 49, 96; extension activity 49, 96; facilitators tip 49, 96;

materials needed 48, 95; page rationale 48, 95; page visual 48, 95; setting the scene 48, 95

missing where you came from 102–103; closure 103; completing the activity 103; extension activity 103; materials needed 102; page rationale 102; page visual 102; setting the scene 103

mountain breathing 87, 88

move your body to lift your mood 97–99; closure 98; completing the activity 98; extension activity 98; facilitators tip 98, 99; materials needed 97; page rationale 97; page visual 97; peaceful place in nature visualisation 99; setting the scene 97

moving on graph 8–9, 91–92; closure 92; completing the activity 9, 92; facilitators tip 9, 92; materials needed 8, 91; page rationale 8, 91; page visual 8, 91; setting the scene 8, 91

moving on podium 68–69, 136–137; closure 69, 137; completing the activity 69, 137; facilitators tip 69, 137; materials needed 68, 136; page rationale 68, 136; page visual 68, 136; setting the scene 68, 136

moving on poem 66–67; closure 67; completing the activity 67; extension activity 67; facilitators tip 67; materials needed 66; page rationale 66; page visual 66; setting the scene 66

moving on takes GUTS[2] see GUTS[2] model

my well-wishes 74–75; closure 75; completing the activity 75; materials needed 74; page rationale 74; page visual 74; setting the scene 74

'name it to tame it' 19

nature visualisation 99

Neff, Kristin 119

Ota, Douglas W. 14

people power 12–13; closure 13; completing the activity 13; facilitators tip 13; materials needed 12; page rationale 12; page visual 12; setting the scene 12–13

Pollock, David 12, 16

Pollock, Michael 12, 16

pros (things that are good) and cons (things that are not so good) 93–94; closure 94; completing the activity 94; extension activity 94; facilitators tip 94; materials needed 93; page rationale 93; page visual 93; setting the scene 93

regulated breathing 87

remember your old place 129–130; closure 130; completing the activity 130; materials needed 129; page rationale 129; page visual 129; setting the scene 129

self-kindness see being kind (kind to self)

Seligman, Martin 52, 117, 122

Siegel, Dan 19, 83

stand like a tree 55–57; body outline 57; closure 56; completing the activity 56; extension activity 56; facilitators tip 56; materials needed 55; page rationale 55; page visual 55; setting the scene 55–56

staying connected 34–35; closure 35; completing the activity 35; materials needed 34; page rationale 34; page visual 34; setting the scene 34

take 5 50–51; closure 51; completing the activity 51; extension activity 51; facilitators tip 51; materials needed 50; page rationale 50; page visual 50; setting the scene 50

talk feelings out 25–26; closure 26; completing the activity 26; extension activity 26; facilitators tip 26; materials needed 25; page rationale 25; page visual 25; setting the scene 25

teachers/therapists 2

thankfulness tree 52–54; closure 53–54;
    completing the activity 53; extension activity
    54; facilitators tip 53; materials needed 52;
    page rationale 52; page visual 52; setting
    the scene 52; thankfulness exercise 54

U-Curve Adjustment Theory 91

Van Reken, Ruth 12, 16
visualisation 99 exploring a feeling visualisation
    23 -24; exploring bravery visualisation 105
    -106; peaceful place in nature visualisation
    99; safe space visualisation 41–42

welcome 1–3, 76–77; closure 2, 82; completing
    the activity 2, 82; extension activity 2–3, 82;
    facilitators tip 2, 82; materials needed 1,
    81; page rationale 1, 81; page visual 1, 81;
    setting the scene 2, 81
wellbeing 92
Wellbeing Boost Game 140–141; closure
    141; completing the activity 141; facilitators
    tip 141; materials needed 140; page
    rationale 140; page visual 140; setting the
    scene 140

what brings me joy? 36–37; closure 37;
    completing the activity 37; facilitators tip
    37; materials needed 36; page rationale 36;
    page visual 36; setting the scene 36
what does my body tell me? 38–39; closure 39;
    completing the activity 39; materials needed
    38; page rationale 38; page visual 38; setting
    the scene 38
what encouraging things can I say to myself?
    43–44; closure 44; completing the activity
    44; facilitators tip 44; materials needed 43;
    page rationale 43; page visual 43; setting
    the scene 43
what's in and out of my control? 45–47; closure
    46; completing the activity 46; extension
    activity 46–47; materials needed 45; page
    rationale 45; page visual 45; setting the
    scene 45; what I can control exercise 46
where are you now? 4–5; closure 5; completing
    the activity 5; extension activity 5; facilitators
    tip 5; materials needed 4; page rationale 4;
    page visual 4; setting the scene 4
who and how? 32–33; closure 33; completing
    the activity 33; facilitators tip 33; materials
    needed 32; page rationale 32; page visual
    32; setting the scene 32